An era in which even if the entire Network connecting our minds were to channel the photons and electrons of our thoughts in a single direction, standalone individuals have not yet been converted to data to the extent that they become discrete components of a larger complex.

A.D. 2030

Other Ghost in the Shell:
Stand Alone Complex novels from DH Press

Volume One: The Lost Memory

GHOST IN THE SHELL
STAND ALONE COMPLEX

#02-04
the original episodes of STAND ALONE COMPLEX

The approximation of mobile media to physical human body started with portable, then wearable terminals, and finally settled to implantable terminals which ushered civilization into a new era where man and machine were no longer separate. Such integration was realized by direct transplanting of communication terminals to the physical body, allowing the body and mind to interact immediately with standard computer and network technology. These implantables gradually took over the outdated portable/wearable technology, to be recognized as the prototype of "Cyberbrain."

After the ever-growing technology introduced the practical utility of micromachines, cyberbrains became both safe and inexpensive. This caused rapid popularization of cyberbrains within countries that had few or no religious restrictions, such as Japan. But the wide prevalence of cyberbrains caused social anxiety: people were exposed to risks of brain-hack because of their neural connection to the entire population using cyberbrains.

The most serious brain-hacking crime was "Ghost Hack," a case where total individuality including past memories and body discretion of a certain person became the subject of the hacker. Various countermeasures were taken, such as the development of numerous protective walls and barriers along with reinforcement of regulations, not to mention security intensification within the neural network system.

But these measures failed to abolish cybercrimes, thus resulting in a rat race: further development of protective walls and barriers, and the emergence of more intelligent and original hackers.

GHOST IN THE SHELL
STAND ALONE COMPLEX

REVENGE OF THE COLD MACHINES

Junichi Fujisaku

Cover illustrations by
Kazuto Nakazawa and Ryouta Niino
English translation by Camellia Nieh

Milwaukie

MOTOKO KUSANAGI—Directs field maneuvers as Section 9's de facto troupe commander. One of the most skilled cybernetic-body operators in the world.

DAISUKE ARAMAKI—Chief of Section 9. Leads with lucid thinking and lightning decision-making abilities.

BATOU—Ex-ranger with an almost completely cybernetic body.

TOGUSA—A rookie hand-picked from the police force by Kusanagi. Aside from his brain implants he has almost no cybernetic modifications.

ISHIKAWA—Information warfare specialist. Served with Kusanagi in the army.

SAITO—A man of few words but exceptional abilities as a sharpshooter.

BORMA—This two-plus-meters-tall behemoth puts his talents to work at information gathering and backup.

PAZ—Strong, silent, cool guy and chain-smoker. Often pairs up with Borma.

TACHIKOMAS—Section 9 is equipped with nine of these sentient multiped mini-tanks.

TANAKA—Resident of the Refugee Zone. Hired as an assassin by the Niihama Wakamatsu Group.

SASAJIMA—Resident of the Refugee Zone, Tanaka's long-time friend.

SHŪZŌ KINOSHITA—Veteran Diet member and leader of the political faction considered the second power of the ruling party.

YŌJI SAKAZAKI—Representative Kinoshita's secretary.

NANA KIRISHIMA—Traffic Division Officer of the Niihama Prefectural Police Ports Precinct.

KARNOV TOYODA—Founding member of leading cybernetics manufacturer Toyoda Chemical.

KIN'ICHI MASUMOTO—Executive Director of Toyoda Chemical. Victim of abduction.

TEGAN YŌ—Mercenary also known as "Twins."

GHOST IN THE SHELL: STAND ALONE COMPLEX
REVENGE OF THE COLD MACHINES

Book design by David Nestelle
Front cover illustration by Kazuto Nakazawa
Back cover illustration by Ryouta Niino
English translation by Camellia Nieh

Published by DH Press
A division of Dark Horse Comics
10956 SE Main Street
Milwaukie, OR 97222

dhpressbooks.com

First DH Press Edition: August 2006
ISBN-10: 1-59582-073-6
ISBN-13: 978-1-59582-073-0

Printed in U.S.A.
Distributed by Publishers Group West

10 9 8 7 6 5 4 3 2 1

Contents

the original episodes of STAND ALONE COMPLEX

#02

魔弾の射手

DOUBLE TARGETS

Chapter 1

Tanaka's prosthetic body ached.

The pain in the index finger of his right hand was especially strong. This didn't make any sense—his index finger was the cheapest cybernetic finger available, and had never included nerve features like the ability to feel pain.

There was probably something wrong with the neural system transmission links between his cybernetic brain and artificial body. Now that he thought about it, he hadn't had a maintenance appointment in more than two years.

What he really needed was a cyberbody exam. If some parts were broken, he could replace them. That was the whole point of having a cybernetic body. Except that . . .

"How can I worry about cybernetics when there's nothing to eat?"

The inhabitants of the Refugee Residential Zones didn't have food, let alone access to cybernetics maintenance care. Right now,

Takana's empty belly was a more pressing issue than obtaining a cyberbody exam.

"Any job prospects?" A voice made Tanaka turn his head. Sasajima was looking at him.

Tanaka would turn thirty-nine this year. If memory served, Sasajima was twenty-seven. They'd known each other for two years. Before they'd wound up at the Zone, Sasajima had been in the same military unit as Tanaka. They'd both been rank-and-file soldiers, outfitted with cheap equipment, and they'd risked their lives together on the battlefield. The two men had experienced hunger together, slept on the same ground, and searched for work in the same humid, dusty room, steaming in the heat of the midsummer sun.

"Not yet." Tanaka was still in the process of looking for work.

He connected his cyberbrain to the help wanted site that was administrated by the camp's refugee network. The image of a stylish chair and table opened in his cyberbrain. By "sitting" in the chair, he completed the process of logging in.

After he'd checked in, a help wanted page appeared and Tanaka began filling out its survey portion. Name, age, cyberparts ratio, special features . . . this process would enable him to zero in on the jobs that best suited him.

But when he finished, all of the jobs that came up were marked "Special Immigrant Labor Permit required" under the heading of Notes. "Special Immigrants" were Asian refugees who had been invited into the country to live in the Zones during the war.

During the last world war, people from various parts of Asia were driven out of their countries by the fighting, and had ended up unable to return to their homelands. At the time, Japan was the only nation that had opened its doors to these exiles.

There were widespread cries of how Japan mustn't abandon its Asian brothers in their time of need. In fact, Japan had been ravaged by the fighting, and in order to rebuild it needed a large body of laborers who would do dangerous work for low wages.

The government provided the refugees with an exclusive residential zone called the Refugee Residential Zone. They initiated various measures to facilitate the refugees' employment, issuing permits to allow them to work under special conditions and granting tax incentives to companies that hired them.

The system was simple: the refugees would provide manpower to Japan, and Japan would provide them with wages. As long as they were physically able, there were plenty of opportunities to work. Those with highly cyberized bodies could do work that was more dangerous but also more lucrative. As a result, all sorts of people began to flock to the Zone—including people who weren't Special Immigrants with work permits. The number of Refugee Zones grew from one to six, and the total number of refugees ballooned to more than two million. Even so, there had always been enough food and beds to go around.

Until the war ended, Tanaka recalled.

Four years had passed now since the armistice. As if to personify the decline in the special demand the war had brought, corporations that had experienced dramatic growth during wartime now scaled down their operations. Demand tapered off in construction, the mainstay of domestic development. As the unemployment rate rose, hostility toward the refugee population mounted.

A portion of every citizen's tax dollars subsidized the livelihood of the refugees, but the refugees were taking their jobs; the refugees were a threat to the lives of Japanese nationals! Such perceptions grew more and more prevalent each day.

With Lower House elections coming up, the government reacted to the unrest by drafting legislation to gradually rescind the protective policies toward the refugees. One of the measures involved limiting the reissue of work permits and reevaluating the labor laws to dramatically restrict the places where refugees could work and the types of jobs available to them.

Naturally, as employment opportunities dwindled, more and more refugees came to rely solely on government assistance. But political pressure caused the government to lower the ceiling on aid programs, and every day the refugees were pushed closer to destitution. Still, the ones who had work permits and were eligible for aid had an advantage: many of the inhabitants of the Zones lived there illegally, unable to qualify for official refugee status. The ones without work permits had no choice but to rely on illicit employers—but those jobs, too, were getting scarcer every day.

Tanaka and Sasajima both belonged to the latter category.

Neither of them were true refugees. They were Japanese citizens, born and raised in Japan. During the war, they'd joined the military and had shipped off to the front lines as part of a clandestine operation. But before they'd fired a single shot, the war had come to a close.

Unfortunately, the fact that Japan had dispatched these units threatened to spark international controversy, so the government decided to cover up their very existence. According to the official story, Tanaka and his fellow soldiers had drowned in the Japan Sea after their ship had capsized during a drill.

Unaware of what had happened, Tanaka and Sasajima had returned to Japan to find that their lives there had been erased. Eventually, they had ended up in the Refugee Zone. That was how they had become refugees.

Today, once again, they would have to search for work in order to stay alive.

Tanaka went through the help wanted ads that came up in his cyberbrain, deleting them one by one.

A segment of the refugee population had committed acts of terrorism against the state, and now there were few employment opportunities for people who couldn't prove their identities. For every one hundred listings he sifted through, Tanaka was lucky if two or three of them weren't designated "Special Refugee Work Permit Required."

After two hours of searching through the employment ads, Tanaka spotted something.

"Ha!" he exclaimed out loud.

Sasajima turned to look at him.

"I found one!" Tanaka offered Sasajima a cable that extended from the nape of his neck. Sasajima accepted it and inserted it into the QRS plug in his own neck. The job information Tanaka had been looking at opened up in Sasajima's cyberbrain.

Job Description: Dismantlers Needed (Military Experience Preferred)

To apply, attach job ID to individual ID and press SEND.

You will receive interview information.

It was the first job he'd seen in two weeks that didn't require a work permit.

"No shit."

"Looks like something we could do, right?"

There was nothing to consider. If they didn't get a job and get some money today, there would be no tomorrow.

Tanaka and Sasajima hit the SEND button without a moment's hesitation.

Chapter 2

"An assassination? Me?"

Daisuke Aramaki, Chief of Public Safety Section 9, furrowed his brow.

Section 9 was a counterterrorist organization that answered to the Prime Minister of Japan, and Aramaki was its commander. Fifteen minutes ago, Togusa had called together all the members of Section 9 for an emergency meeting. Aramaki and the others had gathered in the Tactics Room of Section 9 Headquarters to hear Togusa's report.

Someone was plotting the assassination of Daisuke Aramaki.

"I'm absolutely sure of it." Togusa stood next to a large screen, completely distraught.

"Where did you come across this information?" Motoko Kusanagi, also known as the Major, turned toward Togusa. She was sitting cross-legged in a chair in the front row across from the screen.

"I was investigating the rash of armed terrorist attacks in the

Refugee Zones, monitoring a smuggling organization that deals arms to the refugees in order to pin down the route of the incoming weapons. While I was there, I overheard some very suspicious information."

"Suspicious?"

"The organization had been hired to commit an assassination, targeting someone connected to Public Safety. Apparently they already had a complete dossier on their target, and they were just looking for someone to carry it out. I thought I'd better find out who it was, so I snuck a look at the information when their guard was down."

"And it was the chief, right? You called us all here just for that?" Kusanagi demanded.

" . . . Huh?"

Batou, a huge cyborg with lenses for eyes, chuckled at Togusa's mystified reaction. "Our boss here wrote the book on the rough stuff. People conspire to kill him all the time. We've got our hands full as it is with all the refugee terrorist attacks—we can't go calling meetings over every little plot against the chief's life. This sort of thing is the reason we still call you 'Rookie,' you know."

"You're the only one who calls me that."

"I assume you tracked down the source of the information these smugglers have on the chief?" Kusanagi asked.

"Er, not yet . . . " Togusa faltered.

"Wrong answer. The fact that someone's got dirt on the chief's movements is more critical than the fact that someone wants to kill him."

"I'm sorry."

"Don't waste time being sorry. Do something about it."

Someone thumped Togusa's shoulder. When he turned his head he found himself staring into Ishikawa's bearded face. Ishikawa was a Section 9 veteran who was usually in charge of finding and managing information from the Net.

"Young people dig holes and old people fill them up. I went ahead and tracked down the source."

"Not bad! I'm glad you've got some wisdom to show for your old age!" Batou teased.

"And the source was?" Kusanagi prompted.

Ishikawa turned toward her. "The General Affairs Department of the Ministry of Home Affairs."

Aramaki's gaze grew stern. "They broke through the government barriers?"

Government organizations were equipped with multiple maze barriers and attack barriers to protect against incursions by hackers. The logins and passwords required for external access were changed every two hours, and they were fortified with a tough identity verification system.

Ishikawa used the screen to show them the route the hacker had used to infiltrate the Ministry's security system. The end of the path was a personal marker representing Daisuke Aramaki, labeled *ARAMAKI: Section 9.*

"They snuck in through this route and found out about the meetings the chief is scheduled to attend at the Ministry, etc."

"Does the Ministry know?"

"No. The peephole they used was quite sophisticated. It wouldn't have been easily detected."

"I see." Kusanagi turned to Aramaki. "What do you think? We can easily plug up their peephole, but . . . "

"But there's no guaranteeing that they won't just create a new one, right, Major?" he finished for her.

"Exactly. If this assassin is competent enough to pull down information from the Ministry of Home Affairs, Togusa's concerns may not be entirely unfounded."

Togusa looked up. "Then we'd better decide how we're going to protect the chief, or—"

Aramaki interrupted him. "If an assassin is plotting to take my life, let them plot."

"But, Chief—"

"You can't catch a fish without bait. I'm leaving now for my regular meeting with the Minister of Home Affairs. After that, I have an appointment to meet Mr. Katō of Toyoda Chemical. Apparently he wants to talk to me about cybernetics."

Kusanagi cocked her head quizzically. "Katō of Toyoda Chemical?"

She pulled up the management roster of Toyoda Chemical on the Net and searched for the name. Nobuyoshi Katō, Director of the Administration Department.

"Maybe the Director of Administration of the third largest cybernetics maker in the country wants to do a little whistleblowing," she mused.

"He did say that he wanted to meet somewhere private. But until I talk with him, I won't know what he wants. After that, I intend to return to headquarters. I'm leaving the rest to you, Major."

Aramaki stood up and left the Tactics Room.

"Batou and Saito. Cover the chief," Kusanagi ordered as he departed.

"Roger. We'll look out for him." Saito and Batou headed off after Aramaki.

"The rest of us will follow the hacker's trail and the weapons arteries to track down the assassin. Let's go!" Kusanagi commanded.

Chapter 3

The help wanted ad for dismantlers contained the address of a nonprofit organization. It was called the Niihama Refugee Rescue Association.

Tanaka and Sasajima stood in the NPO's office.

On one wall, an ornate frame displayed the words *Benevolence and Righteousness*, penned in an elegant script. On the opposite wall, a large sign read NIIHAMA WAKAMATSU GROUP.

A fierce-looking man sat across from them on a sofa, gazing at the two men. He didn't look anything like an NPO type. Behind Tanaka and Sasajima, two enormous full cyborgs stood staring down at them. Their arms were as thick as logs, and they clearly had high-output cybernetic bodies with illegal modifications.

The fierce-looking man addressed Tanaka.

"You're Mr. 'Tanaka'?" he asked abruptly.

"Yes."

"Tanaka of the peninsula?"

What kind of question was that? Tanaka thought. But he needed whatever work he could get, so he decided to give an honest answer.

"I was over there with the military . . . "

Without warning, the man got up and kowtowed at Tanaka's feet.

"I'm so glad you're here! I didn't think you would really come!"

The other men followed the man's lead and dropped to the floor.

"I knew you were the only one who could avenge our master. I decided to gamble on the rumors and send you a message over the Net—'Dismantlers Needed, Military Experience Preferred.' But I never really expected that a first-class dismantler like you would really come to our aid!"

Tanaka was baffled. Sasajima seemed to be at a complete loss, too.

"I'm embarrassed to say that there were some fools who saw our message and got the wrong idea somehow, and actually had the nerve to come here looking for dismantling work! We dismantled every last one of them, of course. There were even some imposters who came here claiming to be you! We repaid their insolence by doing a particularly careful job of taking them apart. After a while, we started to doubt whether you would ever really come, Mr. Tanaka. But you did. I'm terribly grateful."

The man bowed his head again.

Thoughts circulated through Tanaka's cyberbrain. *Avenge our master. Dismantlers. They were talking about dismantlers to take apart human beings!*

In crude terms, they wanted a hit man.

Apparently, the scary-looking man sitting across from them was under the impression that Tanaka was a first-rate hit man.

The man raised his head. Their eyes met.

Um, I think you've got the wrong guy, Tanaka wanted to say. But if he did, it was obvious from what the man had just said that by this time tomorrow, their cyberbodies would be dismantled and sold for parts on the black market of the Refugee Zone.

Tanaka kept his mouth shut and allowed the man to continue. The two men didn't speak until they'd left the Niihama Wakamatsu Group's office and were crossing a bridge over the ocean, on their way to the location indicated by the piece of paper they'd been given, along with a single photograph.

"Should we make a break for it?" Tanaka said.

"We can't. If we do, they'll take *us* apart next."

" . . . Yeah."

Tanaka picked up a chunk of concrete and threw it into the ocean. With a *plop,* it fractured the surface of the flowing water below. Ripples formed and dissipated.

Tanaka reached into his pocket and took out the paper and the photograph of their target, a balding man with white hair. The Wakamatsu Group had said that all they had on the man was this picture. They didn't know his name or who he was.

The piece of paper had the address of the location where they were supposed to retrieve the weapon and advance monies.

Arrangements had been made so that when they arrived, they'd be able to determine the man's whereabouts. Apparently, this "Tanaka" was an expert sharpshooter.

Tanaka's cyberbody ached.

Up ahead, they could see the Zone.

"If we stay there, we'll just starve to death in the streets. If we run away and they catch us, they'll break us down into little pieces. Those are our options. So . . . "

"So, you say we do it? Have you ever rubbed someone out, Tanaka?"

"If we don't do it, we're dead. It's like war. Winners take all. If we're going to die anyway, the manly thing to do is go down fighting. Isn't it?"

"Yeah, but . . . "

"We've had nothing but bad luck up until now. This is our chance."

Tanaka moved away from the railing of the bridge. Sasajima followed.

The die had already been cast.

Chapter 4

The Tiltorotor descended through the thick clouds, and the slums of the Refugee Residential Zone unfurled in the darkness beneath them. On the other side, numerous luminous towers stretched up into the sky. When the Tilto got closer, they revealed themselves to be skyscrapers with lights on in the windows.

These were Niihama City's tallest buildings, seen from an altitude of 1000 meters.

The Tiltorotor flew over the network of freeways that interlaced the skyscrapers like a luminous web.

Cold air blew in through the open side-hatch and whipped through Kusanagi's hair. Kusanagi ignored it, concentrating her gaze on a spot on the freeway below.

Togusa observed her from the storage area at the rear of the plane. Her profile was simple and elegant, like that of a beautiful doll.

Kusanagi was a human being, but her entire body was cybernetic apart from her brain and a portion of her nerve cells. The outward appearance of her cyberbody was that of a standard, mass-produced model, but in fact it was composed entirely of special-order parts. Hers was a beauty of functionality, not beauty simply for beauty's sake. Motoko Kusanagi was a doll designed for purely goal-oriented purposes.

The doll looked back at Togusa.

"Yes?" she said.

"N-nothing!" Togusa stammered, abashed. "Er, can you see the chief's car?"

"Clear as day." Kusanagi's gaze returned to the shiny black sedan driving below them on the freeway. "If you want, you can come up here and watch it with me," she suggested.

"No, that's okay. Even if I tried, I don't know if my eyes could follow a car from this height."

Togusa was a member of the Section 9, the cyborg unit under direct command of the Japanese cabinet, but other than his cybernetic brain implants, his body was pure flesh and blood. This put him at a clear disadvantage when he was pitted against criminals with powerful cybernetic bodies. He was able to compensate somewhat with his excellent marksmanship, but even in that regard he still couldn't compete with Kusanagi and the others.

Still, unless something extreme happened to his body, Togusa had no desire to become a cyborg.

If he did, even the scenery he was looking at now would look different to him. Instead of an optical image, he would perceive the light only as numerical values. When he went home and embraced his beloved wife, he'd feel the warmth of her body in digital terms instead of analog. The same would be true of the weight of his darling baby girl when he cradled her in his arms.

Somehow, these misgivings made him hesitant to switch to a cybernetic body.

He supposed he was just old-fashioned.

Togusa turned toward the source of the voice. The Tachikoma sentient tank onboard the Tilto was standing behind him.

The Tachikomas were quadruped mini-tanks equipped with organic artificial intelligence systems that developed continually as they experienced new things. Section 9 had nine such tanks, including the one on the Tilto.

"You stay out of this!" Togusa shot back.

<"You stay out of this"—that's one of your most frequent responses to us, Togusa! You really don't have much affection for machines, do you?>

<Now that you mention it, I get the same impression!>

<Me too, me too!> Tachikomas strategically deployed at other locations joined the conversation by cybercomm.

"Tachikomas! You're supposed to be keeping watch! Concentrate on your job!" Kusanagi barked.

<Yes, ma'am!>

<I'm sorry, Major,> the Tachikoma onboard apologized dejectedly.

"Togusa, you shouldn't let the Tachikomas mess with you," Kusanagi said.

"I know, I know . . . so, are we just going to continue monitoring the car from up here?" Togusa asked.

"No, that won't be necessary. Batou and Saito are in the car with the chief, Paz is four vehicles behind, and Borma's standing by in a parking lot up ahead. Besides, I've sent the other eight Tachikomas to the sites along the freeway that Saito pinpointed as possible sniping points. We have other work to do."

"Finding the person who commissioned the chief's assassination?"

"Exactly. If we just want to head off the assassination, all we have to do is prevent the assassin from obtaining his weapon. But if we're dealing with a pro, he'll come up with an alternative strategy to go after the Chief. The most effective defense is to strike at the source—the person who hired the assassin."

"I get it. I suppose if we arrest that person, it'll also serve to deter anyone else plotting against the chief."

"Precisely. The first step is to identify the weapon they intend to use."

"Let's hope it doesn't get ugly," Togusa said. He removed his gun of choice, a Mateba, from his hip holster and checked its magazine. The six-shot chamber was fully loaded with high-speed armor-piercing bullets with heightened firepower for anti-cyborg combat. He closed the magazine and re-holstered the gun.

"I guess I don't have to worry with you here, Major," he remarked.

<*Don't forget about me!*> the Tachikoma reminded him.

"Oh, right, I forgot."

<After all, I'm more suited to combat than you are!> In the storage area, the Tachikoma stomped its four feet loudly on the floor of the Tilto.

"Okay, okay! I'm counting on you!"

<Then take off my safety devices! Come on, Major, pleeeease?> The Tachikoma implored the Major to remove the safety devices covering its frontal grenade cannons.

"Overruled," Kusanagi responded coolly.

<Pretty pretty please?> the Tachikoma persisted. *<Launching grenades raises our experience ratings!>*

"Our goal is to find out what kind of weapon is being issued to the assassin. No rough stuff. When we find out what we want to know, we'll withdraw. You'll obey orders, or you'll be scrapped."

The Tachikoma froze. *<Being scrapped means that my existence would be terminated?>*

"That's right."

<Mmm, I don't think I would like that.>

"Then do as you're ordered. That's all."

"Sixty seconds until drop-off point," said the inorganic voice of the android operator on board.

"Togusa and Tachikoma, prepare for descent," Kusanagi directed.

"Roger." *<Roger!>* chorused two voices, human and machine.

The Tiltorotor veered away from the skyscrapers below and toward the outskirts of Niihama City. The lights below became sparser as they flew over a residential area reminiscent of the previous century, filled with low-rise mixed-use buildings and apartments. The variable rotary wings of the Tilto began to pivot upward from their horizontal orientation into a more vertical landing configuration, allowing it to drop straight down through the sky. When it neared the rooftops of the apartment buildings below, it curbed its descent and hovered midair.

"Let's go!" Kusanagi commanded, leaping down towards the rooftop five meters below. Togusa and the Tachikoma followed suit.

As soon as they had disembarked, the Tiltorotor whizzed off into the night sky.

Chapter 5

The streetlamps cast a bluish-white sheen on the surface of the road.

Two human shadows interrupted the light. They belonged to Tanaka and Sasajima.

They'd come to pick up their weapons. According to the map on the slip of paper they'd been given, the strip club that was their destination was just a little way beyond the next intersection.

Both men stared straight ahead as they walked in silence.

They'd come this far. There was no turning back.

They crossed the intersection, leaving the residential area. After about five minutes, they came to a commercial district. Signs indicated that there was a subway station nearby. Rows of small shops congregated around the station. Most of them had their shutter doors drawn.

The two men turned right at the shopping street and entered an alley lined with mixed-use buildings. The strip club they were looking for was just up ahead. The garish light of the neon sign on the wall by the entrance shone a blue-and-pink glare on the pavement.

Tanaka reached a hand toward the bar's thick wooden door and gave it a forceful push. An onslaught of loud hard rock escaped from inside, assailing them.

"What a racket," Tanaka muttered.

"Is this really the place?" Sasajima wondered, surveying the interior.

A syrupy stench hung in the air. Glitzy multicolored lights flashed in their eyes. On the main stage, a half-naked woman clung to the obligatory pole. The men in the bar leered as she hypnotized them with her bump and grind.

Approximately 70 percent of the seats were occupied.

Various pairs of men and women sat on stools next to the wall, their cyberbrains wired together and their expressions vacant. They were probably engaging in cyberbrain sex. Not all of the pairs were heterosexual—there were same-sex pairs of both genders. That was the sort of establishment it was.

Tanaka and Sasajima approached the bar at the back of the room. The bartender eyed them as he waved his cocktail shaker in the air.

Before either man had a chance to speak, they were given mugs full of an amber liquid. They exchanged glances, then looked back at the bartender.

Drink, the bartender's eyes ordered them. His sharp gaze informed them that disobedience wouldn't be tolerated.

Tanaka and Sasajima tipped the liquid down their throats.

It was warm and its consistency was absolutely repulsive.

Automatically, they stopped drinking. Their gazes met. *Do we have to?* their eyes asked each other.

Tanaka looked at the bartender.

The bartender continued to glare at him.

Tanaka shut his eyes and downed the drink in a single drag.

The liquid that flowed down his throat felt almost slimy.

Why did they have to do this?

His glass empty, Tanaka gave the bartender a reproachful look.

"Hey . . . " Sasajima said to Tanaka.

"Yeah?" Tanaka looked at him.

Sasajima was staring fixedly into his mug.

Tanaka looked into the mug in his own hand, and then looked back at the bartender. The bartender turned away from them and went back to tending to the other customers.

Tanaka looked at Sasajima, and he could tell that they were both thinking the same thing.

"Is this for real?"

"I guess we'd better go find out."

Tanaka set his mug down on the counter and began to walk away from the bar. Sasajima did the same.

The bottom of the mugs on the counter bore a terse inscription: BROKEN TOILET.

The bar had two bathrooms. One of them had a sign on the door that read OUT OF ORDER. Tanaka turned the doorknob and slipped quickly inside. Sasajima followed, closing the door behind him. Instantly, the raucous music from the bar grew faint.

The room was dingy.

The grimy toilet was cracked.

This bathroom was out of order, all right.

The tiles on the walls were broken, and fallen shards surrounded the toilet.

A naked light bulb dangled from the ceiling. They could hear the low hum of a fan emanating from behind the net of the hinged air vent.

Tanaka opened the small window on the opposite wall. Outside, the wall of the next building was close enough to touch.

There was no sign of a weapon anywhere.

Had they been tricked? Tanaka glanced at Sasajima.

Sasajima was looking at him, his expression dubious. He seemed to be thinking the same thing.

That was when it happened.

They heard a noise from the ceiling.

Tanaka looked up. The net of the air vent was gone, leaving a dark hole in its place. In fact, the entire ventilation fan was gone.

A man's face peered through the hole. It was the bouncer who had been standing by the front door. He lowered a rope ladder down into the room, then disappeared again.

Tanaka and Sasajima exchanged glances once more. There was no backing out now. Tanaka gave Sasajima a nod and grasped the rope ladder.

Gingerly, he stepped his feet onto the flimsy ladder and slowly began to climb. When he stuck his head through the air vent and into the crawlspace, he could see nothing but darkness.

The space was only about fifty meters high. He could feel a complicated object near him consisting of cables, pipe, and a metal frame. Approximately five meters away from the air vent, he could see a single bright spot in the darkness.

Tanaka drew himself up into the crawlspace and crept towards the light. Behind him, Sasajima was climbing the ladder.

"Pull up the ladder and replace the ventilation fan," a voice said. It came from the same direction as the light. Sasajima did as he was told.

Tanaka continued to crawl slowly through the darkness. Beneath them, he could feel the vibrations of the hard rock blasting downstairs.

Now he could make out the source of the light. There was an opening in the ceiling above them, allowing light to spill in from the second floor.

Tanaka climbed up through the opening.

The second-floor room consisted of a perfectly ordinary-looking office. There were four steel desks in the center of the room, and the walls were lined with metal cabinets.

The bouncer was removing a guitar case from one of the cabinets.

Sasajima crawled up out of the floor and stood next to Tanaka.

"This is the specialty item that's been arranged for you," the bouncer said tonelessly, setting it down on one of the desks.

Tanaka and Sasajima eyed the guitar case.

"I hope it's compatible with your lenses. The Wakamatsu boss made a personal request. I owe him plenty of favors, so I went out of my way to get you the very best piece available." The bouncer opened the case.

"A Steyr," Tanaka murmured.

"Yeah. A Steyr SSG. An Austrian sniper rifle with bolt action. Most have plastic stocks, but this one is an army-style competition model, with a Walther diopter and a wooden stock. That can come in handy, you know."

The bouncer was right—the wooden stock could serve as an effective weapon in close combat situations. Tanaka didn't anticipate engaging in hand-to-hand combat with a sniper rifle, but it was better to be safe than sorry.

"The reason I chose this piece is that the joint between the receiver and the barrel is a whole 57 mm thick. See how the receiver covers almost the entire chamber? This stabilizes the ballistic trajectory inside the gun, guaranteeing you an accurate shot . . . 'course, I'm sure I don't need to explain all this to you."

"Yeah," Tanaka said without conviction. "So, this is what we'll be using to . . . "

"That's right," Sasajima confirmed hoarsely.

With the rifle in front of them, the reality of what they had to do became suddenly much more immediate.

The bouncer placed the rifle's 7.62 mm cartridges and a miniature memory device on the table.

Tanaka picked up the device. "What's this?"

"See for yourself."

Tanaka did as the bouncer said, using a wire from his cyberbrain to connect to the device. A map and a clock opened in his cyberbrain. A cursor appeared in the middle of the map data, followed by the word "TARGET."

"That's your guy. We'll continue to send you information as we obtain it. Your job is done when that target has been eliminated."

"I see."

"According to the latest update, the target is currently at the Ministry of Internal Affairs."

"The Ministry of Internal Affairs!" Sasajima exclaimed inadvertently.

Tanaka took the photo out of his pocket and stared at their target's face.

"So, this man isn't just some low-life. He's a big-shot politician or something?"

"I don't know. All I know is he's your target." With that, the bouncer opened the door.

The message was clear. He had no more to tell them. It was time for them to leave.

Probably, he really didn't know.

Tanaka touched the Steyr SSG lightly and ran his fingers down the barrel to the small of the stock. His life depended on this weapon.

Tanaka closed his eyes and imagined it. Looking for a spot to hide. Waiting patiently for his target to appear. Shooting the target. Running away.

"It'll all be over in just three seconds," he whispered and looked at Sasajima.

Sasajima nodded in agreement and picked up the rucksack that had been left next to him.

The metallic sound the guitar case's clasps made as they snapped shut was surprisingly loud. Or perhaps it only seemed that way.

Tanaka reached down with his right hand for the guitar case, then changed his mind and used his left instead. Aside from life itself, a sniper's right index finger was the most valuable thing he possessed. *It wouldn't do to use it for such a trivial purpose,* Tanaka thought, lifting the guitar case in his left hand.

His arm communicated the weight of the guitar case and rifle to his brain.

A feeling of strength welled up inside of him.

Tanaka shook himself for a brief second, then stepped resolutely out into the world, the guitar case in hand.

Chapter 6

<Ishikawa, we've confirmed the assassin's method of attack.>

A cybercomm from Kusanagi reached Ishikawa at Section 9 Headquarters, where he was monitoring the hacker who had infiltrated the Ministry of Internal Affairs' server.

Kusanagi and Togusa had gone out to track down the vendor who was providing the weapon. Apparently, they were done.

Ishikawa took his cigarette out of his mouth and dropped it into his empty coffee can.

"Yeah? What is it?"

<A sniper attack.>

"Sniping, huh? That's awfully orthodox of them. What kind of weapon?"

<A Steyr SSG.>

"They're not messing around. It might be tricky pinning down the smugglers."

<We can worry about that later. I want you to deploy the Tachikomas in a two kilometer radius of the chief and raise the alert level.>

"Two kilometers? Isn't that a bit of a large spread?"

<With an ordinary sharpshooter, one kilometer would be plenty. But not with the guy we're up against.>

"Who're we up against?"

<Have you ever heard of a mercenary called Masaki Tanaka, a specialist in sniper assassinations?>

"Yeah, I've heard of him. He's well known in Honduras and in the Taipei area, right? If that's the guy you're talking about, even a two kilometer radius focus might not be enough." Ishikawa called up the information confirming Aramaki's whereabouts on the monitor. "For the moment, the chief's still inside the Ministry."

<Where's the parking lot located?>

"It's close to the front entrance."

<And Batou and Saito's location?>

"They're standing by in the lobby."

<Got it. When you've determined all of the possible sniper attack locations within range of the front entrance, I want you to send them to Saito.>

"Roger. But, Major . . . we can fend of the sniper attack, but the assassin will escape. We should do something to zero in on him. For example, we could post information to the server I'm monitoring that the chief's plans have changed. The hacker will convey the information to the sniper, right? Then we can use a reverse-trace to determine his location." Ishikawa pulled a cigarette out of his shirt pocket. It was his last one.

<That might be a plan. Where's the chief headed next?>

"He's supposed to meet a guy called Katō of Toyoda Chemical, the cybernetics maker," Ishikawa responded, lighting his cigarette.

<Location?>

"ALI-98372. The Newport Hotel."

<Let's shake them up a bit, shall we? I'll notify the chief. You take care of the sniper points, please.>

"Roger. I'll set up a dragnet over the server."

Ishikawa turned back to the monitor and immersed himself in the Net.

Chapter 7

Aramaki had come to the Ministry of Internal Affairs to meet with the Minister of Internal Affairs and his cohorts. They had been conversing for two hours.

The ministers had gathered here to discuss what to say at the upcoming Diet session when they were questioned regarding the ever-mounting armed terrorist attacks by refugees. As a faction, they needed to draft a unified response, and Aramaki had to make time in his busy schedule to attend.

Indeed, the refugee crime wave was intensifying day by day. There had been several riots, albeit small ones. Aramaki was concerned that there might be agitators at large who could pour fuel on these little flare-ups, causing them to sweep through society like wildfire.

Luckily, Section 9 existed to investigate and curb that sort of activity. As the group's leader, Aramaki had to be decisive in his actions and unfaltering in his convictions.

Of course, the Chief had many enemies. This was to be expected, given that he was the commander of a counter-terrorist organization. But right now, he was more concerned about the ministers in this room.

They'd ceased discussing the refugee issue, the meeting's original agenda, after just fifteen minutes. Now, the topic they seemed most interested in was the golf tournament that would take place in three days for retired party members. This topic elicited much more impassioned discussion than the refugee issue had, as they debated whom to invite, how the players should be paired, and the order of play.

To them, it was important to hold meetings, but the content of the meetings was of secondary relevance.

In Kusanagi's opinion, this was an everyday practice among politicians intended to project the semblance of doing work, and she advised Aramaki not to waste his time with them.

But Aramaki felt that observing the interactions of the Diet members during these casual encounters offered a glimpse into the hidden workings of the political arena. After all, politicians had dealings beyond the assembly rooms and Diet sessions. It was important to keep tabs on their cash flows and mistresses—the real political system functioned at night. For these reasons, Aramaki felt that attending these ostensibly useless meetings was an essential part of his duties.

The meeting drew to a close when it was almost time for the Minister of Internal Affairs's next appointment.

"Batou. I'm leaving now."

<Roger.>

Aramaki sent a cybercomm to Batou, who was waiting in the lobby, then proceeded to the bank of elevators in the Ministry's hallway.

One of the elevators was already on its way to his floor. When it arrived, its iron doors slid open to discharge a swarm of Diet members.

"Greetings, Aramaki. Are you here making a pilgrimage to the Minister?" one of them called out to him.

It was Shūzō Kinoshita, the representative of the Kinoshita faction of the ruling party. He was a veteran Diet member who was known as the opinion leader of the ruling party's second power. He'd entered politics as the secretary of the late Labor Minister Tadayama, who had been mysteriously murdered amid rumors of collusion with cybernetics makers. Kinoshita had gone on to build strong ties with the cybernetics industry and had climbed the political ladder to his current post.

"Just my regularly scheduled report. You're working late, aren't you?" Aramaki watched out of the corner of his eye as the herd of politicians funneled into a chamber labeled "Conference Room."

Kinoshita smiled. "Just a little study meeting, that's all."

Quickly, Aramaki took stock of the meeting's participants. He recognized several of their faces as belonging to affiliates of the Labor Ministry.

Just then, Aramaki became aware of someone staring at him. He turned to encounter a young man with a piercing gaze.

"Sir, we'd better get going . . . " The man said to Kinoshita—perhaps he was Kinoshita's secretary.

"Yes, you're right. Excuse us, Aramaki." Kinoshita followed the others into the conference room.

The young secretary shot Aramaki a sharp glance. The eyes that peered out from behind his rimless glasses were fox-like.

Aramaki openly returned the man's gaze. It seemed to him that he'd seen these eyes somewhere before.

"Sakadoki! What are you doing?" Kinoshita's voice called from the conference room. So that was the young secretary's name.

"Coming." Sakadoki shot Aramaki one last look before closing the door behind him.

Aramaki was alone now and the hallway was completely quiet.

His portable terminal went off, shattering the stillness.

"Aramaki speaking."

<Chief. Are you done meeting with the Minister of Internal Affairs?> It was a cybercomm from Kusanagi.

"I just finished. I'm about to head to my next appointment."

<Katō of Toyoda Chemical, right? I wanted to have a word with you about that.>

"A word? What is it?"

<Well . . . >

Two men sat on a sofa in the Ministry's lobby.

Batou and Saito.

Both of them were clad in black suits, superficially indistinguishable from those of security guards. But the workers who crossed through the lobby plainly averted their gazes when they saw the two men and gave them a wide berth as they made for the revolving door at the entrance.

"Does it seem to you like we're getting the cold shoulder?" Batou wondered as he observed them.

"It's better than having them approach us," Saito responded.

"True. But still . . ." Batou looked Saito and himself over. "Don't you think we look way more like thugs than security guards?"

Saito looked at him. "Maybe you do, but I don't."

"Yeah, right." Batou muttered, giving Saito a once-over. Saito's head was completely shaved and he wore a patch over his left eye. He glared sharply out at his surroundings like a hawk searching for prey.

"The chief's back," Batou said as the elevator doors opened and Aramaki stepped out. Batou exited the lobby and headed toward the parking lot. In order to reduce the odds of being sniped as much as possible, it was important for Aramaki to get into the car in a place that was relatively sheltered.

As he settled into the driver's seat of the black sedan, Batou cybercommed the Tachikomas.

"Tachikomas. Any unusual activity at your positions?"

The Tachikomas were currently deployed at the various points from which a sharpshooter might attack the front entrance of the Ministry.

Even in a two kilometer radius, it had been possible to narrow down the possible locations based on the data Ishikawa had sent.

<*Coast is clear!*>

<Here, too!>

One after another, the Tachikomas messaged in.

"Okay . . . so I guess our work here is done?" Batou asked himself. He turned the steering wheel and began to drive the car toward the front entrance.

Aramaki was just stepping out through the front door, with Saito covering him. Batou got out of the car and opened the rear door, and he and Saito escorted Aramaki to the car, protecting him from either side.

Saito kept his stern gaze trained on their surroundings.

"Let's go," Batou said, climbing into the driver's seat.

Saito grunted his assent and climbed into the back seat, next to Aramaki.

The black sedan glided away from the front doors of the Internal Ministry.

In the front seat, Batou glanced at Aramaki through the rear-view mirror. "Next stop, ALI-98372, the Newport Hotel?"

"No. There's been a change of plans."

"A change of plans? We're not going to the Newport Hotel?"

"I've decided to indulge in a little fishing trip instead."

"Fishing?"

"That's right. I want you to reach point ERT-0987 in two hours—drive through the city."

Aramaki sent Batou the address. Point ERT-0987. The address indicated the east gate of the Refugee Residential Zone.

"We're going to the Zone?"

"It's the ultimate sniping location. Surrounded by ocean with no obstacles whatsoever," Saito muttered.

At that, Batou looked at Aramaki in the back seat again and smiled. "You sure are a wily old ape. You're going to lure them into shooting at you, aren't you?"

"Let's get rolling."

"Roger." Batou stepped on the accelerator.

Chapter 8

Tanaka was on the roof of a skyscraper, preparing to stake out his target. There were no obstacles between him and the front entrance of the building in question. This was the ideal position.

Tanaka thought back to his military stint; how when he'd first joined up, he'd wanted to become a sharpshooter. He'd even undergone training. His reason was a simple one: he'd seen a movie about sniping.

The targets they had practiced with were just dummies. It was all about the endurance test of waiting and waiting. After you'd made your shot, you had to beat a swift retreat, whether or not you hit your mark. Those were the requirements.

That was more than ten years ago.

Through the reticle of the scope, the front entryway swayed quietly with his breath.

Except that . . .

"Aren't we practically two kilometers away?" Sasajima pointed toward the building as he peered at it through binoculars.

Tanaka withdrew his eye from the scope and called up their location on the map information in his cyberbrain. The distance was 2.7 kilometers.

"I guess it is pretty far . . . " Tanaka mumbled.

"I checked on the Net—it said that normal sniping distances range from 900-1000 meters."

"It'll be all right. The heroes in movies make shots from distances like this."

"But that's in the movies! Those are special effects!"

Tanaka got into position behind the gun, lying flat against the concrete.

"We'll never know if we don't try."

"Huh?"

He could see a flag flapping in the wind atop the building in the scope.

"That flag up on the roof there. I'm going to shoot it."

"That's impossible!"

"Don't you know anything?" Tanaka pointed at the scope. "Sniper rifles are designed to hit the target you see through the reticle, as long as you don't move them."

"That seems like a pretty far-fetched—"

"Don't worry. This is just practice."

Tanaka centered the reticle on the flag.

Every time he breathed, the image rocked.

He held his breath. The image became still.

His right index finger squeezed the trigger.

A 7.62 mm bullet sprang forth from the gun. The Steyr SSG jerked in Tanaka's hands and the bipod stabilizing the gun danced on the concrete, trying to break loose.

"Ow!" The impact to his right shoulder sent a jolt through Tanaka's cyberbody.

Regaining his composure, Tanaka peered into the scope again at the flag.

It was flapping in the wind, just as before.

"Where did the bullet go?"

"Over there." Sasajima pointed, looking through the binoculars.

Far off to the right of the flag, a glass windowpane was broken.

"Oh . . . "

Even Tanaka had no idea how to explain how the bullet might have flown in that direction. The influence of the wind, a bad angle when he shot, the reticle needing adjustment, miscalculating his target . . . the possibilities were endless.

"Okay! I've got it!" Tanaka exclaimed, rising to his feet.

"Really?" Sasajima asked haltingly.

"Now we know the rifle's quirk. We can't hit our target from here. Let's move out."

Sasajima lowered his binoculars and turned toward Tanaka. "Really?" he asked again.

"Yes. Now get a move on!"

"Okay. You don't have to get mad!"

Reluctantly, Sasajima followed Tanaka's instructions. He began to unscrew the bolts fastening the rifle's bipod to the concrete.

Tanaka looked at the building through Sasajima's binoculars.

As he was watching, the man who was their target emerged from the building's front door.

He recognized the face from the data the Wakamatsu Group had provided. When he killed this man, their work would be done.

But it was important not to rush things.

If they made another mistake, they might provoke a counterattack next time. Tanaka and Sasajima knew the people who had commissioned the assassination. That was reason enough for someone to come after them.

The man who was their target got into a car. They were on the move.

"Their next stop is the Newport Hotel, right?"

Just as he spoke, the data in his cyberbrain was overwritten. Apparently, the man had changed his plans. Someone must be pulling this information from a server somewhere. Tanaka could tell because the data was accompanied by the unique static generated when a hacker ripped through a barrier. There was a link to the data on the new destination.

Time and coordinates. One hour from now, at a site near the east gate of the Refugee Residential Zone.

"The east gate of the Zone. That's right by our roost."

"That's good. When we're done, we can go straight home."

"No, it's *not* good. If we pull a job like this in our own neighborhood, we'll arouse suspicion!"

"True . . . "

"When this job's over, we have to get the hell out of Niihama."

"What?"

"If we pull this off, it won't be long before they have another assignment for us. And on and on forever—until we screw up, that is. We can't keep living in the Niihama Zone. We'll have to flee to the Kantō Zone."

Tanaka put the binoculars in the sack and pulled its drawstring tight. Then he put away the Steyr SSG and the bipod Sasajima had unfastened, fitting them into the guitar case and latched it. He picked up the guitar case and headed toward the stairs.

Sasajima trailed after him. "I wonder what it's like in Kantō?"

"I don't know," Tanaka answered as he walked. "From what I've heard from guys who've been there, there's a big hole where there used to be solid land a long time ago."

"Wow."

"There isn't much work—mostly dredging up things that are still salvageable from the sunken city. Of course, since they still haven't done much redevelopment, there's probably more work out there than here in Niihama."

"Huh. Maybe our lives will be better there."

"Yeah. I'm going to work my ass off and buy a new cyberbody."

" . . . I guess we won't have to do stuff like this anymore."

Sasajima's words made Tanaka stop walking.

"I don't know. If there's nothing else, we'll have to take what we can get. With the 1.5 million we're making on this job, we might have enough for new cybernetics, and we might be able to actually find decent jobs . . . "

"Yeah . . . I'm happy for you. But I don't know what I'll do—I don't have a cybernetic body." Sasajima hung his head.

Tanaka laid a hand on Sasajima's shoulder and peered into his face. "That's not what I'm saying, Sasajima. You'll get a cyberbody, too. We'll find jobs together."

"Tanaka . . . " Sasajima smiled.

"We've been together all this time, haven't we? In Honduras, and in Shanghai . . . we came through all of it together."

Sasajima nodded.

"C'mon, let's go. Our target's on the move, and we only have an hour," Tanaka urged.

"Yeah."

They ran down the stairs.

Chapter 9

The words "Refugee Residential Zone" appeared on an exit sign of the Niihama metropolitan freeway. Batou checked the sign and veered left. The car moved into the exit lane.

"We'll arrive at our destination in two minutes," Batou called toward the back seat.

"Right on schedule," Aramaki responded from the back.

Batou glanced at the rear-view mirror.

Despite the fact that an assassin was plotting his demise, Aramaki was the very model of self-composure. He had a lot of confidence in Section 9's members.

Aramaki checked his watch.

"What about Mr. Katō?"

Batou checked the car's monitor.

"He's on the bus, just as planned."

"I see. He must be almost there by now."

The car was approaching the bridge that led into the Refugee

Zone. Inside, Saito was working to ascertain the sniper's position. He called up a map of the Refugee Zone on the monitor in the car's cockpit. Meteorological information and other data was superimposed over the geographical data.

"Shit, that's impressive!" Batou exclaimed from the driver's seat.

"Watch the road, fool. I just layered the information with my Hawkeye."

Saito was Section 9's sharpshooter, and the Hawkeye was the satellite link system hidden by the patch he wore over his left eye. It was configured to retrieve data from weather, communications, and various other satellites, and to convert that data into a format optimized for sharp-shooting purposes, instantaneously displaying it in a visual format.

Normally, human beings have approximately two hundred thousand photoreceptor cells. The Hawkeye had 1.5 million—eight times the visual strength of the naked eye. It didn't just magnify objects like using a telescope; normally, objects at a distance appear blurry to the human eye for optical reasons, but the Hawkeye allowed them to be viewed with absolute clarity.

Once he'd used the Hawkeye to gauge a shot, all Saito had to do was use his cybernetic left arm to shoot his mounted rifle.

Saito's prosthetics were tailored to his profession. His left eye and arm, and their connective tissues, were artificial. In order to preserve the minute sensory perceptions that couldn't be reproduced by prosthetic technology, Saito's other organs, including his right eye and arm, were flesh and blood.

More than anything else, Saito's greatest asset as a sniper was the perceptiveness and patience gleaned from his years of experience.

"Normally, the wind would be a factor in the Refugee Zone. But at this hour, wind and updrafts aren't really a problem. The only real challenge right now is gauging the shot in the dark."

"Because it's hard to see the target?"

"Yeah. But if he has cybernetic eyes with light-gathering mechanisms, it won't be an issue."

"Where are the ideal points to snipe from?"

Saito marked three locations on the map. One was at the top of a small hill, four hundred meters from their destination. The next was the roof of a seven-floor building in the Refugee Zone. It, too, was four hundred meters away. The last point was on the arch of the bridge that led into the zone—a three hundred-meter distance.

"If it were you, where would you shoot the chief from?" Batou asked.

"I would do it from here."

"Huh?" Batou was mystified. Saito was pointing to a point across the bay in Niihama City, nowhere near the other three sites. Even Batou could see that there were far too many obstacles between the target site and the spot Saito was indicating. "Could you really snipe someone from out there?"

"It's a distance of fifteen hundred meters. There's a bridge and a parking lot gate in the way—but I could do it."

"Okay. I'm sure you could."

"There are two priorities that we snipers always have to keep in mind: can we be sure of hitting our target, and can we be sure of making a clean getaway," Saito explained flatly, perusing the sniper points displayed in his cyberbrain. "At the three points I showed you, you wouldn't have any trouble hitting your target. But if you were worried about making your escape, you'd want to be as far away as possible or you might not make it."

"According to the major, the sniper we're dealing with is quite the virtuoso." Batou said to Aramaki. "Are you sure you don't want to rethink this?"

"Don't be ridiculous," Aramaki said, still staring straight ahead. "We've got him right where we want him—this is no time to cut bait! Proceed according to plan."

"Just checking. Major, can you hear me?" Batou messaged Kusanagi.

<I'm listening.>

"We're almost at our destination. I'll do what I can to prevent the Chief's head from acquiring a new ventilation system. The rest is up to you."

<I know.>

Kusanagi activated her Type 2902 thermoptic camouflage, melting into her surroundings, and began to search for the sniper.

When she found him, she would still have to keep her distance. If she got too close, he might detect her presence.

Like in swordplay, timing was everything.

If she moved too quickly, the sniper might notice her and run away. If she was too slow, Aramaki could lose his life.

It was a battle against time.

But even when she found the sniper, she couldn't intervene immediately.

<Ishikawa. Have you tracked down the hacker yet?> She messaged Ishikawa back at Section 9 headquarters.

<Almost.>

Ishikawa had laid a dragnet to catch the hacker when he came for the information Aramaki had overwritten at the Ministry. When Aramaki had changed the location of his meeting with Katō, the hacker who had been monitoring the server saw that the data had been updated and had crept in for a peek. Ishikawa had tacked a thread to the snoop in order to trace his movements.

This was a hacker capable of penetrating the formidable barrier of a government agency, so Ishikawa had to exercise the utmost caution in tracking him down. He was taking it nice and slow. It was tedious work—following the thin thread and searching for traces for the hacker in the infinite reaches of the Net.

He was almost there.

<My target's within sight. When I apprehend the hacker, I'll send a bogus message to the sniper from the hacker's address. When he gets it, you should see a reaction of some kind.>

"You should be able to trace the hacker's location, right?"

<Yeah. There are only a limited number of spots from which someone could snipe the east gate of the Refugee Zone. The sniper could be at one of the points Saito indicated.>

"Send Tachikomas to the first three points. I'll cover the one Saito chose."

<We don't have much time. I'm counting on you, Major.>

"I know."

When she was finished communicating with Ishikawa, Kusanagi broke into a run.

Where was the sniper?

The black luxury sedan with Aramaki inside was crossing the bridge into the Refugee Zone.

Batou messaged in. *<Major. We'll arrive in about twenty seconds.>*

"I know."

Kusanagi messaged Ishikawa at headquarters. "Ishikawa!"

<I found the hacker. I'm sending a cybercomm to the sniper!>

"Hurry!"

Kusanagi drew the Sebro M5 from her hip holster.

Ishikawa sent the sniper a phony communication.

Every second felt like an eternity.

Aramaki's car pulled into a parking lot.

A car was visible in the halo cast by the headlights.

"Is that it?"

When they were just five meters from the car, Batou hit the brakes and pulled to a stop. He twisted his body to look back into the back seat.

"Hey, Pops. Are you sure you want to go out there?"

"This is my job."

When he heard the resolution in Aramaki's voice, Batou stepped out of the car. The early morning air was chilly.

Saito climbed out of the passenger's side and cast a stern gaze over the surroundings.

Batou moved toward the rear door and reached for the handle.

The latch opened with a *clack*.

He opened the door slightly, then stopped.

"Chief . . . "

Through the narrow crack, Aramaki stared out at him, his gaze stern. His eyes bespoke an iron will.

"Open the door," Aramaki said.

"Okay, okay."

Batou swung the door open wide.

Slowly, Aramaki emerged from the car.

The balding, white-haired man appeared in the reticle.

The sniper's right index finger was about to squeeze the trigger of the Steyr SSG.

Just then, a transmission flashed into his cyberbrain.

A cybercomm from Ishikawa reached Kusanagi.

<*Major*>

"Roger!"

Kusanagi looked at the sniper.

His right hand moved.

Without hesitation, Kusanagi pulled the trigger of her Sebro M5.

○ ○ ○

Under the cold sky, a shot rang out at the eastern gate of the Refugee Residential Zone.

Aramaki turned toward the direction from which the shot had resounded.

Kusanagi watched as the high-velocity armor-piercing bullet from her Sebro M5 blew off the sniper's trigger finger.

At the same moment, a bullet from a hidden assailant blasted Masaki Tanaka's head to smithereens.

Tanaka watched as the 7.62 mm bullet from the Steyr SSG he was holding pierced the skull of an older sharpshooter whose name he didn't even know.

Chapter 10

Kusanagi arrived at the eastern gate of the Refugee Zone riding in a Tachikoma.

Aramaki got out of the car and came and stood next to her.

Kusanagi looked at his feet. "Looks like you've still got your legs," she remarked.

"I don't intend to die anytime soon," Aramaki responded.

"Paz has escorted Mr. Katō of Toyoda Chemical to a safe location, just as we planned. By contacting him directly instead of by cybercomm, we managed to keep the hacker in the dark," she reported.

"A primitive, but highly effective method," Aramaki remarked. "So the sniper who had a bead on me got his head blown off?"

Kusanagi shrugged. "Yes. Someone blasted it off at almost the precise moment I took off his trigger finger to keep him from shooting you. The man who was with him committed cyberbrain suicide when he saw that Tanaka was dead."

"So there was more than one sniper."

"Yes. When we conducted a broader search of the area, we found this."

Kusanagi handed Aramaki a plastic bag. Inside was a photograph and an empty shell casing. When Aramaki saw the photograph, he let out a groan.

"What's this?"

"I suppose that was the other sniper's target."

"So the sniper's target was the other sniper."

The photograph in Aramaki's hand was a picture of Masaki Tanaka, the veteran sharpshooter.

"Do we know the whereabouts of the sniper who shot Tanaka?"

Kusanagi shook her head. "We searched in the direction the shot came from. We found holes where a bipod had been fastened on a rooftop fifteen hundred meters away—that was probably where they were."

"What about the hacker?"

"Ishikawa and the others are hot on his trail."

"I see."

In a slum of the Niihama cyberbrain district, the man had already stopped breathing.

The room was in a multi-purpose building. Its floor was littered with cyberbrain terminals, and the dead man lay in their midst, half buried in the devices.

Ishikawa knelt by the body and inserted a connector into the plug at the nape of the man's neck.

"His brain's fried . . . "

"His brain?"

Borma, who was investigating the room, looked up at Ishikawa.

"Must have been a Thought Bomb."

"Wherein a certain thought pattern is set to trigger the desire to commit cyberbrain suicide, eh?"

Paz, who had been investigating another room, joined them. He was carrying a small memory device. "Hey. It looks like this fellow left a detailed record of his communications with his employer."

"A communications record? Who was he talking with?"

"I'm analyzing it right now. The ID belongs to—Yōji Sakazaki."

Ishikawa let out a surprised shout. "Representative Kinoshita's secretary!"

Aramaki was in a room at the Interior Ministry.

Representative Kinoshita was just about to leave for a lunch meeting with the Diet members of the Kinoshita Faction.

"Aramaki—"

"Representative Kinoshita. Is Mr. Sakazaki available?"

"Sakazaki? What do you want with him?"

Aramaki walked straight toward Kinoshita, staring fixedly into Kinoshita's eyes. "Your secretary, Mr. Sakazaki, is under investigation as an accessory to murder. However, we're unable to determine his location at this time. We thought that you might know where he was, Mr. Kinoshita."

Kinoshita's expression darkened.

Aramaki continued, unperturbed. "Actually, we're gathering information about a sniper attack on a party who was investigating the illicit flow of funds between a certain politician and cybernetics manufacturer. We've found evidence that your secretary, Mr. Yōji Sakazaki, was connected to the sniper."

"My employee, Sakazaki, you say? How terrible! I'm sure that the party in charge of the investigation must be quite frightened to have someone plotting against his life!"

"Public Safety Section 9 doesn't abandon an investigation over something as mundane as an assassination attempt. We'll round Sakazaki up in no time."

Aramaki noted the change in Kinoshita's complexion.

"I'm sure I'll be coming to speak with you again. Let me know if you come up with anything you'd like to tell me."

Aramaki left the room. Kusanagi was waiting outside.

"What?"

"You were awfully soft on him."

"Without Sakazaki's testimony, we can't pin anything on Kinoshita. I could have made a big scene in there, but without enough evidence, he might slip through our fingers. Our priority right now is finding Sakazaki."

Kusanagi shook her head.

"It turns out Sakazaki is the son of Minister Tadayama, of the Health, Labor, and Welfare Ministry."

"Minister Tadayama?"

"Yes. Apparently, after Tadayama's death, he went to live with his mother's side of the family and took their last name."

"I see. Please continue investigating his whereabouts."

Aramaki turned to leave, but before he had gone far he stopped and looked back at Kusanagi.

"By the way, what's the word on the other sniper, the one who shot the sniper Yamazaki hired?"

"From the shell casing we found, we know he was using a Steyr SSG, the same gun as Masaki Tanaka. We found out that he obtained the weapon through the organization that hired him, the Niihama Wakamatsu Group. Unfortunately, we missed the chance to apprehend him red-handed."

"The Niihama Wakamatsu Group?"

"A small-potatoes crime syndicate. Apparently, the late boss was taken out by a sharpshooter, so they hired a sniper called Takana to avenge his death. The man they hired was a Tanaka, but he wasn't Masaki Tanaka. Here's the really moronic part: The Niihama Wakamatsu Group tracked down the sniper who'd shot their boss, but the only thing they knew about him was what he looked like."

Kusanagi took out the photograph of Masaki Tanaka.

"This photo was all they had to go on. Then they found out that their man was getting data from the Internet and was changing location to follow his target."

"That was when I changed my schedule at the Internal Ministry, eh?"

"Yes. You get the gist: they sent their sniper—Tanaka—after their foe, who would have to show up at the designated location. In other words, the Niihama Wakamatsu Group tried to hire

Masaki Tanaka to rub out their enemy: Masaki Tanaka. In fact, the other Tanaka they hired ended up taking out Masaki Tanaka, so ultimately they achieved their revenge. It's not a case that's worth our energies."

"You're right. Pass the Tanaka case off to the police."

"Roger."

Chapter 11

Tanaka was looking at the Help Wanted ads on the Net.

Actually, he wasn't so much looking at them as staring past them.

His mind was elsewhere. His was thinking back over the events that had transgressed since the sniping contract.

He and Sasajima had left the Niihama Refugee Residence Zone and fled directly to the Kantō Zone without retrieving the reward money. If they had stayed, he figured, they would have ended up dismantled and tossed into the ocean.

There were no rewards to be reaped from killing people.

The ongoing battle to survive was no more than an extension of the war.

He had learned afterwards that the older sharpshooter had been a sniper in the last World War, with quite an impressive killing record. Coincidentally enough, he'd also had the same last name as Tanaka.

Their lives had been very similar.

The only difference was that the other Tanaka had made a name for himself as a hit man. But Tanaka himself had once been fairly well known as a mercenary. Of course, that had been a long time ago. During the World War, Tanaka had sniped scads of soldiers. His name had inspired fear. But one day, he'd faltered during a battle and was taken prisoner by the enemy. That was how he'd lost his right index finger.

That was the day Tanaka's career as a sharpshooter had been cut short.

When he'd returned to peaceful shores, he'd found no work suited to a man who knew nothing but war. He'd returned to the military, and was shipped off to the peninsula as a foot soldier.

It was a mystery to him how he'd been taken for the legendary Masaki Tanaka and hired to assassinate Masaki himself.

Perhaps he would be next. The thought had crossed his mind.

But somewhere inside, Tanaka had the sense that with Masaki dead, Tanaka himself had also lost his life.

Yes.

Tanaka the sharpshooter was dead.

"Hey, how about this job?"

Sasajima's voice pulled Tanaka back to reality.

"It's another ad for dismantlers . . . "

"No more dismantling work."

"Then how about this one? They're looking for laborers for subterranean work. Says they'll provide cybernetic bodies."

"They'll provide cyberbodies for free?"

Working underground sounded arduous, but it had to be better than killing people.

Tanaka's body still ached.

If he got a new cyberbody, he would finally be rid of the pain.

When the thought occurred to him, Tanaka entered his name in the application form without a moment's hesitation.

Shōji Tanaka.

the original episodes of STAND ALONE COMPLEX

#03

タチコマの恋

FIRST LOVE, LAST LOVE

Chapter 1

<Comrades! If memory serves, it's been 216 hours, 48 minutes and 28 seconds since I met her.>

One of the Tachikomas was addressing the others in the lab at Public Safety Section 9.

It was an unusual-looking Tachikoma.

It had a two-tone, black-and-white paint job and a revolving light on its head. It even sported a Niihama Prefectural Police Department decal on its rear pod. The grenade launcher at its mouth had been replaced with a white bullhorn.

<That's a really wild getup! Are you playing dress-up?>

<Oh! Oh! What's going on?>

<Did you have an interesting experience of some kind?>

<Who are you talking about?>

<You say "if memory serves," but your memory is backed up by searchable records. I don't see any reason why it wouldn't serve, do you?>

<I want a new experience, too!>

All at once, the other Tachikomas began to clamor.

<Comrades! I understand your sentiments precisely! But now that I think about it, if we synchronize our data, the memory will become shared, eliminating the need for me to tell you my story!>

<That's true. But considering the possibility that a recounted memory might have a different impact from the pure memory itself, I think you should tell us about your experience. That way, we can confirm whether or not each of us really interprets the experience differently. What do you think?>

<Very true! Okay, listen carefully, everyone!>

<Yeah, yeah! Hurry up and tell us!>

<Okay! Let's see. I was with Batou, pursuing a suspect . . . >

<Tachikoma! He went that way!>

<Leave it to me!>

Batou and I were at the Niihama wharfs to chase down a bomber who used a kind of cyberbrain virus called a "Thought Bomb."

The Thought Bomb is a weapon in which the occurrence of a certain negative thought is set up to trigger an escalating urge to end one's life, and the victim invariably commits cyberbrain suicide within forty-eight hours! This bomber was a mass murderer who had infected eighty-two Net freaks with Thought Bombs while they were in Net space, driving them to cyberbrain suicide.

Using the Net, the killer sought out victim after victim. Apparently, his favorite prey of all was the net bounty hunters who were trying to track him down! If we let this go on, it would cause widespread fear of using the Net, creating major disturbances to not only business but to everyday life! So the major ordered Batou and I to conduct a certain operation . . .

<I know what you're talking about! We helped, too, right?>

<Yeah! The one where we created pseudo-personalities to act as decoys!>

<So that's what that experiment was for!>

<Comrades! I haven't finished my story! If you want to hear the rest, don't interrupt me!>

<Okay, okay! Sheesh!>

Anyway, the perp infected the pseudo-personality I created with a Thought Bomb. But to me, the concept of death doesn't exist! He accessed the Net to find out what had happened to the Thought Bomb that had never gone off, and Batou ran a back-trace and zeroed in on his whereabouts.

Batou and I rushed over to Wharf 13.

<Tachikoma! Get in front!>

Just as Batou had commanded, I sped off at top speed to circle ahead of the perp and cut him off from the other side. It wasn't easy—a truck pulled out in front of me, and there was a container in my way—and by the time I caught up with the perp, he was about to leave the wharf!

<Stop or I'll shoot!>

I readied my right chain gun. I aimed it at the perp's feet and let 'er rip! DADADADADA! Chunks of concrete flew everywhere!

If I'd aimed right at him, I'd have blown his legs right off. So I went easy on him and aimed five centimeters in front of him. I figured that would surprise him and get him to stop running.

But instead of stopping, the perp came right out into the street!

Right then, a Minipat came barreling down the road. It looked liked it was going to hit the perp!

In a panic, I dashed in! Somehow, I just managed to get between the perp and the Minipat! The impact was awesome! The Minipat went up my body and flipped over sideways. The perp was between my legs. He seemed unharmed, but he was laid out on the ground in a faint.

So I left the perp there and went to check on the Minipat. It was lying on its side, all scratched up, and its front windshield was smashed.

<Oh, noooooo! Are you dead?> I found myself shouting.

I reached out and gave it a shake, but there was no reaction at all!

Then a door opened, and a policewoman came out.

"What a piece of junk!" Those were the first words out of her mouth. She kicked the Minipat's body.

I looked up the policewoman's identity. Snooping into the police's server is a piece of cake, of course. It took less than two seconds. Her name was Officer Nana Kirishima, and she worked for the Port and Harbor Traffic Division of the Niihama Prefectural Police.

It seemed like the most diplomatic thing to do was to apologize, so I did. After all, the Minipat was totaled!

<I'm sorry.>

But the policewoman's response was ice cold. "Oh, great. A programmed apology. This is why I hate robots!"

I interpreted this as a challenge to our kind. Of course, we are robots in the broadest sense of the word. But while robots only obey commands, our autonomous AIs endow us with independent decision-making abilities, and in that sense, I don't think we *are* robots!

Naturally, I tried to explain.

<When I said, "I'm sorry," it was a decision I reached on my own, not a programmed response. The subject I was chasing did run out into the road—but it was your Minipat that almost mowed him down, so you were the one who should have stopped, don't you agree? Traffic laws obligate you to be alert to obstacles in the road. Considering that you work for the Traffic Division, you could probably be charged with dereliction of your duties for that sort of violation. But I reasoned that getting wrapped up in all that would be disadvantageous to both of us, and in our society, often these situations can be resolved if the victim apologizes. That's why I said I was sorry—>

"Enough. I hate chatty machines!"

To be completely honest, it was a real shock. I felt like I'd been personally invalidated!

Officer Kirishima seemed worried about the condition of the Minipat. I think this didn't stem from any affection for her vehicle, but rather her concern over its function as a tool, and her own responsibility in that regard.

You know why? Because she'd already had to submit seven letters of apology just this month!

<You seem to be injured . . . are you all right?>

The policewoman was cradling her right arm. Red blood was trickling down it.

"It's nothing. Leave me alone."

For some reason, I felt rejected.

That was when Batou arrived.

"Hey, Tachikoma! Why haven't you secured the subject?"

Looking back on it now, I should have done just as Batou said. It was negligent on my part. But for some reason, I was just overwhelmed by the feeling that I needed to check on the totaled Minipat first.

Batou reached out to put a cyberbrain lock on the bomber, who was still lying on the ground. But at the same moment, the man opened his eyes. When he saw me, he froze—it was like his cyberbrain had crashed!

Batou connected up to the perp's brain to see what had happened.

"Cyberbrain suicide. The bastard used one of his own Thought Bombs."

<*What a bone-headed screw-up!*> one of the other Tachikomas said.

<*It wasn't a screw-up. The bomber had that thought bomb set up from the beginning. Even Batou didn't know about it. There was nothing we could have done!*>

<*Hmm . . .*>

All at once, the other Tachikomas tilted to one side and stared at the Tachikoma who had been telling the story.

<*W-w-wait! You guys don't think that I killed him, do you?*>

< . . . .>

There was no way to read the faces of the other Tachikomas, but if multiped tanks were capable of wearing a dubious expression, they were doing so now. That was what the Tachikoma's AI told it.

<In any case, just listen to the rest of the story.>

Batou and I decided to withdraw. Just then, Officer Kirishima asked, "Are you two Prefectural Police?"

<We're Pub—>

"Yeah, we're from the First Investigations Division."

Batou really thinks on his feet. Right when I was about to tell her we were from Public Safety Section 9, he cut in and fooled her into thinking we were Prefectural Police.

After all, nobody really knows how our organization is structured or what kind of weapons we have at Section 9. Actually, the fact that nobody knows that stuff is probably our greatest weapon of all!

Then Batou told Officer Kirishima, "Hey lady, no offence, but this case is under our jurisdiction. You can write that in your letter of apology if you want. We're sorry about your Minipat. Hey, Tachikoma, set it upright, will ya?"

<Yes, sir!>

Immediately, I did as Batou ordered. I didn't want to cause it any more damage, so I turned it over very gently.

But Minipats are a lot more delicate than we are, and its body was really beat up. Its windshield and headlights were broken, too.

I felt just terrible about it! My AI was exhibiting a really strange reaction. I guess something must have happened in my neurochips.

"C'mon, Tachikoma. Back to HQ."

<Yes, sir.>

Batou and I left the site. Looking back, I was beset with feelings of guilt.

<Yeah? Go on!>

<What happened next?>

The other Tachikomas urged the storyteller on.

<Okay. So when we got back, I assumed I'd synchronize data with the rest of you like we always do. But for some reason, I was the only one who didn't get synchronized that time.>

<WHAT? No fair!!>

<How come you get all the breaks?>

<Well, it was the Major's decision. I guess they succeeded in forcing the Thought Bomb into an endless loop in my pseudo-personality, but they weren't able to completely delete it. There was still a possibility that the bomb might still be active somewhere in my thoughts. So the major said that I should be "stand alone" until we could be sure that the bomb had been disarmed.>

<I see!>

<The major sure is smart!>

<I think so, too. Then they gave me a new task. The pseudo-personality had been deleted, but in order to make sure it wasn't still affecting me, they sent me on an external assignment.>

<An external assignment?>

<Lucky!>

<Where'd you go?>

<You'll never guess . . . >

<Where?>

<The Port and Harbor Traffic Division of the Niihama Prefectural Police!>

Chapter 2

The assignment was for one week. I was presented as an "Artificial Intelligence-Equipped Traffic Directing Robot" that the prefectural police would be trying out on a temporary basis.

In order to make me look the part, they gave my body a black-and-white two-toned paint job, stuck on a Niihama Prefectural Police sticker, and even put a revolving light on the antenna part of my head. Later, Batou told me that it wasn't really necessary to do all of that, but that the Red Suits at the crime lab were having fun with it and got kinda carried away.

The major took me to the Harbor Precinct, which is a branch of the Niihama Prefectural Police Department.

The Niihama Prefectural Police were the capital city police until just recently, so some of the commanders and officers there are awfully self-important and proud. When they pay a visit to a precinct station, the officers there avoid them like the plague.

The Harbor Precinct is right by the Prefectural Police Department. For geographical reasons they tend to handle a lot of international crimes and violent cases, so they end up doing a lot of joint investigations with the Prefectural Police.

For that reason, the other precincts make fun of the Harbor Precinct, calling them a division of the Prefectural Police. I learned this from Togusa.

When I got to the Harbor Precint, the Prefectural Police were leading a special investigation of the abduction of the executive director of Toyoda Chemical, and they'd set up their investigations headquarters at the precinct.

The crime had taken place three days before, in the early morning, at the home of Kin'ichi Masumoto, executive director of Toyoda Chemical.

According to their housekeeper, a pair of masked men showed up suddenly at the house, dragged Mr. Masumoto out in his pajamas, and absconded with him in their car!

The housekeeper called the police right away, but all they could find was the footage of the two masked men on the security cameras. They didn't uncover a blackmail letter or any other clues as to who the attackers were or what they wanted.

Forty-two hours after his abduction, the Mr. Masumoto was picked up walking along a highway in the next prefecture, two hundred kilometers from his home.

The kidnappers had used a cyberbrain lock to immobilize Mr. Masumoto, and his sensory organs had been shut down, so he had no idea what had happened to him. When he'd come to, he'd found himself standing on the highway.

Of the dominant cybernetic body makers, Toyoda Chemical has a really large market share; they're a multinational corporation with manufacturing and distribution bases in a number of countries. They've put a lot of resources into public service projects, too, such as providing free used and refurbished cybernetics to refugees. Because they're such a high-profile entity, there's more than enough reason to suspect corporate terrorism. As the abduction of the executive director of a major cybernetics manufacturer constitutes a serious incident, the prefectural police took command of the investigation, setting up shop at the Harbor Precinct since Toyoda Chemical is headquartered in that precinct.

But that case doesn't really have anything to do with my being sent on assignment to the Traffic Division, so let me get back to my story.

The major said she had to take care of some procedural formalities, so she went to talk to one of the big bosses of the Traffic Division and sent me to the garage. Apparently, my role there was to be more that of a police vehicle than a police officer. I wasn't being deployed as personnel; I was being deployed as equipment!

<Hello! I'm a Tachikoma!>

I introduced myself, but there was no response.

This was no wonder, because the wireless patrol vehicles in the garage—patrollers, for short—weren't outfitted with language or voice output devices. They didn't have sophisticated artificial intelligence systems, either.

Apparently, they have a basic artificial intelligence device that coordinates with their GPS systems for self-navigational purposes, but fundamentally they were meant to serve as machines for human usage, and their abilities are tailored to that end.

Also, with that black-and-white two-toned paint job, it's patently obvious to anyone who sees them that they're police vehicles. This convention dates back to olden times and represents an authoritarian system; the idea was that the police's presence would act as a deterrent to criminals. When humans encounter these symbols, it creates a sort of repressive reaction in their brains, reminding them not to commit crimes. Of course, the same is true of us: we learn through experience how to differentiate between what kind of behavior is acceptable and what isn't.

I linked up to their external connectors to have a look at their data, but all they had were businesslike records of stuff like how far they had traveled, what their patrol routes were, who their drivers were, etc. Talk about bland and humorless! But I guess that's just how the police are.

Right when I was in the middle of connecting up to various vehicles, accumulating experience points, *she* showed up. Her Minipat came rolling into the garage.

The dent in her side was the one she'd gotten from crashing into me the other day. Her engine was making a funny sound, so I knew it wasn't all better yet.

I was truly happy to see her again. After all, I never thought we'd see each other again! But the first words out of Officer

Kirishima's mouth when she opened the door were, "Oh, it's *that robot* again."

I don't think Officer Kirishima liked me very much.

I guess it made sense. After all, while it's true that human beings' memories deteriorate over time, it had been less than twenty-four hours since the first time we'd met. And I was the one that had caused the damage to the Minipat. It was only natural that she still retained her first negative impression of me.

"*This* is supposed to be my new partner?" Officer Kirishima said, looking at me.

As a rule, the officers of Niihama precincts perform their rounds and duties in pairs. But the policewoman who had been Officer Kirishima's partner had left the force to get married, and Officer Kirishima had been on her own since then.

When she saw me, Officer Kirishima phoned the Traffic Division from the garage extension.

"Chief, what's this all about?"

Just then, the major showed up. "Are you the Officer Kirishima that will be working with our Tachikoma?"

"Tachikoma?"

"This robot," the major said, looking at me. I don't like being described as a robot, but of course the major can call me whatever she wants.

"We want the Tachikoma to take part in operations at this station for a week so that we can examine the records in its AI. I've cleared everything with the top brass already. I appreciate your cooperation."

"Who are you?"

"Prefectural Police Officer Kusanagi—I'm the Tachikoma's educational supervisor."

The Major extended her right hand. Officer Kirishima shook it courteously.

"Oh! Your hand's warm! Pardon me, but I thought . . . " the Major looked surprised.

Officer Kirishima pulled her hand away. "Never mind that. Why is it being assigned *here*?" Her voice was beginning to sound slightly hysterical.

But the Major remained calm. "I know that this is an inconvenient time, with everyone so busy with the special investigation of the abduction of Toyoda Chemical's Mr. Masumoto. I'm afraid, however, that we have orders from the top."

The major shrugged and looked at me. "See you later, Tachikoma. Be a good police officer for a week!"

<Yes, Ma'am!>

She didn't like it, but Officer Kirishima had no choice but to accept me. I guess that's one of the drawbacks of living in a hierarchical society.

That day, the Minipat was being repaired, so I spent all day in the garage learning about prefectural police work from Officer Kirishima. Gradually, she became slightly less frosty toward me. On the morning of the third day, the Minipat's repairs were done, so I got to go out for the first time!

As she climbed into the Minipat, Officer Kirishima, too, seemed glad to be relieved of doing nothing but paperwork. "Tachikoma, we'll be conducting our regular patrol of PC-1113. Repeat it back to me." I detected a cheerful undertone in her voice.

<We'll be conducting our regular patrol of PC-1113. Right, ma'am?>

"Don't embellish." Officer Kirishima drove the Minipat out into the streets of the precinct.

I followed right behind her. Then I drew up next to the Minipat and asked, *<Um . . . so where are we headed?>*

Officer Kirishima opened the window and looked out at me. "When we leave the wharf, we'll enter the city. We'll take the high route."

When she said "high route," she was talking about the freeway system. Of course, normally when *we* say "high route" we mean leaping from rooftop to rooftop and building to building. But apparently the police don't usually travel that way.

So for a while, I drove next to her on the freeway. That day, the sky was clear and blue, and it was a perfect day for a drive. The wind felt wonderful!

<The wind felt wonderful?>

<It's not fair!>

<Yeah! How come the rest of us don't get to go for drives!>

The Tachikomas listening to the story began to clamor.

<Hold on, everyone!> The Tachikoma on top of the container said. *<The drive wasn't an end in itself, I just happened to get to take a drive because of my assignment! It wasn't something that I requested—so please don't hold it against me! Besides, things got really rough after that!>*

<Things got rough?>

<What happened?>

<I bet it raised his experience points.>

<Wow! I want to hear about that!>

<Yeah, tell us! Tell us!>

<I was about to tell you, when you went and derailed my story! Well, anyway, we got on the freeway and headed toward the wharf. When we got off the freeway and arrived at the wharf, there weren't any major incidents, it being daytime and all. There were four container trailers illegally parked in no-parking zones, and one minor collision at an intersection. The real trouble happened afterward, when we were patrolling the city—>

Chapter 3

There's an area in the Port Precinct that looks out over all of Niihama City. It still retains the flavor of the Nanjing Town neighborhood that was founded there by Chinese immigrants more than one hundred years ago, and its atmosphere and colors are a little bit different from the streets we're used to.

Now that I think about it, none of us had ever been to that area before.

In the olden days, it really was an immigrant neighborhood, but now it's more like a sort of theme park. The buildings and the clothes of the passersby all have an exotic quality, reflecting the styles of Shanghai in the 1920s. Even the smells in the air are straight out of that era.

Of course, it seems odd for a place to be modeled on Shanghai when its name is Nanjing Town. Human beings can be so imprecise!

Officer Kirishima went deeper and deeper into the neighborhood. All I could do was follow along.

Everyone was looking at us. Both she and I were clearly out of place there.

<*Um . . . what are we supposed to do here?*>

"You'll know in a minute. This is the place."

Right in front of us, I could see a sign indicating the entrance to an underground parking area. Officer Kirishima drove her Minipat down the ramp.

The ramp curved gently as it descended into the ground. It was more like a loop than a curve, actually, with an eight-degree angle.

It was a privately run parking facility with four levels, built right under a national highway. These parking facilities are configured so that police vehicles can automatically enter them for free, so Officer Kirishima was able to drive right in without stopping. But not me.

<*Please take a parking ticket.*> the terminal at the entrance said to me.

<*Excuse me, but I'm a police vehicle . . .*>

<*Please take a parking ticket.*>

<*Officer Kirishimaaaa!*> I called. But she'd already driven off ahead and wasn't looking my way.

Well, that was no surprise. After all, she'd already said that she hated me.

<*Could you* please *let me through?*>

<*Please take a parking ticket.*>

<*You leave me with no choice . . .*>

I knew that those simple terminals don't have speech recognition faculties so there was no point trying to reason with it further. I would have to hack into it to get through.

I went into the data inside the parking terminal and pulled down the record of one of the cars parked there. Then I rewrote the record so that it would show me as being "access granted."

But the data only included records of the cars that were currently parked and cars with fixed parking spots, so I was unable to determine Officer Kirishima's location.

You know, I bet if those parking systems were linked up to the police Net, it would be really useful for crime prevention. But because of privacy considerations, we can only access such information *after* a crime's already been committed.

Besides, crimes can occur anywhere. So maybe there'll never be a way to establish a perfect crime prevention system. It definitely won't be possible for as long as the police only act after incidents have already happened. At Section 9, we move to strike at the root before a crime takes place, nipping it in the bud. That way, unless it feeds into another incident, there's no need for the police to get involved in every little case.

If the police and Section 9 coordinated their roles really well, we could stamp out crime in no time. But both systems are governed by human beings, so there are always various entanglements to contend with, and nothing ever works the way it should.

I bet if they just left everything to us, we'd do a good job of eradicating crime.

To put it in extreme terms, if there were no humans there'd be no crime in the first place—like the robot revolts human beings imagine in their C-level sci-fi movies!

If you think about things in the most practical, efficient way, it's easy to come up with answers. But human beings always insist on the contradictory "human way" as a primary condition, sending our reasoning cycles into an endless loop. This is what human beings refer to as being "troubled."

Luckily for me, I'm not a human, so I discussed the matter machine to machine, and persuaded my counterpart to see things my way. Of course, I used coercion as my method of persuasion.

Actually, it was Batou who taught me that if the other party is unable to see reason, you have use force.

Then I had to find Officer Kirishima, who had driven off ahead of me.

<*Officer Kirishima? Where are you?*>

They'd built this parking lot underneath a national highway, so it was awfully big. It was hard to know where to begin looking.

<*Good grief! Where the heck did she go? Talk about inconsiderate!*>

Twenty-four seconds after I'd begun searching for Officer Kirishima, I encountered two suspicious-looking men. They emerged from an elevator that descended into the underground parking lot from above.

One of them had one of those cyberbodies that has "illegal-modifications" written all over it. He had beefy arms and was embedded with external cylinders.

The other was a pot-bellied, middle-aged fellow.

<*Gee, I wonder what line of work you guys are in,*> I muttered.

The two men hadn't noticed me yet, so I activated my thermoptic camo so that I could get closer without them seeing me.

The big guy looked around and said, "So where're the goods we're supposed to fetch?"

The middle-aged guy said, "All I know's the license plate: MNB-LKJ 389."

"Just the license plate? That's it? You don't know what the car looks like, or what color it is, or anything?"

"Nope. We're better off not knowing any more than we need to know, right?"

"For crying out loud! This job's more trouble than it's worth! What's inside, anyway?"

"I don't know. But they've already paid our advance. We're supposed to deliver the designated car to the designated place. That's all."

From their conversation, I gathered that the two men were couriers. It didn't sound to me like the cargo they were moving was likely to be anything legit. It stank to high heaven!

The men began to inspect the license plates of the cars in the parking lot, one by one. I decided to head them off by finding what they were looking for before they did. I knew that the license numbers of all of the cars in the lot had to be recorded in the terminal at the entrance.

I searched the information I'd swiped from the terminal.

MNB-LKJ 389.

I found it instantly, of course. It was parked on level 4B.

The two men were still searching the first level. They had cyberbrain implants to interface with their cybernetic bodies, but they didn't know how to effectively harness the powers of the Net. That's how it goes!

I ran into Officer Kirishima down on level 4B.

She'd gotten out of her Minipat and was leaning over one of the parked cars. It was a big SUV. It was also the car that the two men were looking for—the one with the license number MNB-LKJ 389.

The car was parked with its rear bumper facing out, and Officer Kirishima was examining its trunk.

<Officer Kirishima! There's something I need to tell you . . . >

She turned and looked at me as if I'd called her out of a trance.

"Just a moment. I just found a car that's been reported stolen."

She began to inspect the car. She flattened herself against the ground and began to look for something on the car's underbelly with a dental mirror.

<What are you looking for?>

"You know that stolen cars are often used for car bombings, don't you?"

<Yes.>

"I'm looking for a bomb."

<A bomb?!>

" . . . But there doesn't seem to be one here." She stood up.

I let out a deep sigh of relief. Not literally, of course, since we don't have lungs. But that's the human expression that best describes how I felt.

<Um, is looking for bombs part of our duties at the Traffic Division?>

"No. It's just an old habit of mine."

<Habit?>

"Before I was assigned to the Port Station, I used to work in the Investigations Bureau at Niihama Central Station. "

<Oh, you were a detective! Why are you working in the Traffic Division now?>

She paused for a moment. "It's a long story. You're probably not aware of this, but police work is bound up in a lot of outdated practices."

I learned later that the Traffic Divisions of precinct offices are also known as "Waiting Rooms," because when policewomen are transferred in from another precinct, their first assignment is always the Traffic Division. For men it's the Community Affairs Divisions. Community Affairs officers do stuff like manning police boxes and parking lots, but even if you were a detective before you were transferred, you always get assigned to Community Affairs until a position opens up in Investigations.

So for officers who're used to doing more important jobs, it's probably the police equivalent of being shunted off to a subsidiary in the corporate world. They say it's to allow them to get acquainted with the community as a foundation for investigations work, but that's just an excuse.

For women, it's the Traffic Division.

Officer Kirishima didn't really talk about it herself, but I suppose that it must seem pretty insulting for a detective from Investigations to be reduced to making rounds as a traffic cop.

Even if she was an ex-detective, though, as a traffic cop there wasn't much more she could do here.

<What now?> I asked her.

"I'll report it to headquarters."

<*But I saw some men who're looking for this car.*>

"What men?"

<*They said something about delivering some goods.*>

"Goods?"

Officer Kirishima eyed the car's trunk. It had a remote lock with a QRS plug interface.

<*I might be able to open it,*> I suggested.

"What?"

<*It's not too hard to pick this sort of lock–you just have to find the right waveforms to open it.*>

"Just a moment—"

I wanted to satisfy my curiosity as to what was in the car's trunk. That is to say, I wanted to satisfy my greatest longing, that was a function of the very core of my being. I extended a hacking cable and connected it to the QRS plug.

I knocked on the key program.

The car responded: *cannot open*.

Tell me, I whispered.

The response was the same. *Cannot open*.

I repeated the process.

The dialogue between two machines is a simple one, with one response for every question. But the difference between talking with machines and talking with humans is that with machines, a vast quantity of interactions can be conducted simultaneously, within the space of an instant.

They say that a long time ago, there was a human named Shoutoku Taishi who was capable of listening to ten of his disciples talk at once. We, on the other hand, can carry on dialogue with tens or hundreds of thousands of machines at once. But that's because humans and machines operate in different time frames.

My dialogue with the car's electronic lock took less than 0.5 seconds. I won it over, and it clicked open.

<See?>

Proudly, I lifted the lid of the trunk.

<Whoa! What's this?>

There was no answer. Officer Kirishima was stunned.

I don't blame her; inside the trunk was a brain shell, hooked up to a life-support system. We had no clue whose it was!

I extended a cable and connected to the brain shell—partly because I wanted to find out whose it was, but also because the brain looked like it probably knew things beyond my ken. You can't blame me for being curious!

But it only lasted for a brief moment.

Just then, the two men who were looking for the car came down from the level above us. They saw us just as we saw them. In a flash, they pulled out sub-machine guns. Not just little self-defense-type handguns—really deadly looking SMGs! An ear-splitting roar echoed through the lot as they let loose a barrage of 9 mm parabellum fire!

Quickly, I leapt in the way to protect her. But of course, I can't move faster than a bullet travels. When the shots hit my body, she was already hurt.

The side window of the Minipat was shattered and her body was peppered with holes. Next to it, Officer Kirishima lay wounded on the ground.

<*Oh, no! Are you okay?*>

As I turned my attention to Officer Kirishima, the sound of a car's engine filled the air.

I looked up. The two men had closed the trunk and were driving off in the stolen car.

Its rear wheels spun wildly and it rocked sidewise two or three times, hitting the cars on either side of it, then came surging straight at me!

<*OH, NO YOU DON'T!!*>

I didn't budge. If I'd moved, the car would have hit her.

Just when the car was about to slam into me, it veered off toward the exit, barely skimming by me. It tore clear through the chain link gate.

I listed as the sound of the engine faded away in the distance.

<*Hey, Officer Kirishima . . . Are you okay?*> I asked her.

If the visual information I'd gathered was accurate, her body had taken a total of seven bullets!

"I'm okay . . . " she said, getting up.

Then I saw that she wasn't bleeding from the points on her chest and left arm where the bullets had hit. She rolled up her left sleeve. The flattened bullets were lodged in her flesh.

"Lucky they weren't high-speed armor-piercing shells," she said.

She got out a knife and dug the smashed shells out of her arm. They made a little clinking sound as they fell onto the concrete.

Officer Kirishima's left arm was cybernetic.

The artificial skin and muscle fiber of cybernetic bodies is usually comparable in strength to that of a flesh-and-blood body. There are special cases, like the Major with her titanium skeleton and ultra-dense muscle fiber, but you don't see that sort of thing every day.

But Officer Kirishima's cyberbody was the same kind as the major's—super high-performance—even though superficially, it didn't look very different from an ordinary flesh-and-blood body. The bullets had broken her artificial skin, of course, but the specialty fibers underneath had effectively dispersed and absorbed the impact of the shots, minimizing her injuries.

Considering how negative her attitude was toward robots and machines, it came as a surprise that Officer Kirishima had a cybernetic body!

Shakily, she pulled herself to her feet.

"So, I suppose I ought to thank you now?"

<That would be nice . . . >

"A robot that likes to be thanked. Okay. Thank you for shielding me."

<You're welcome!>

Little by little, the distance between us was diminishing.

When I say distance, I'm not referring to physical distance, but rather the time involved in prioritizing decisions based on empirical thought—psychological distance, to put it simply. When something beneficial happens to a human being in association with a certain entity, he or she tends to integrate that entity into their "in group" domain classification. For Officer Kirishima, I was now a part of that domain.

In other words, she was beginning to accept me.

I was pleased. <*My conversation with that brain shell got cut short, but it belongs to a Mr. Masumoto, Executive Director of Toyoda Chemical,*> I told her.

The instant she heard Masumoto's name, Officer Kirishima's expression changed.

"Masumoto . . . "

<*I wasn't able to verify its I.D., but that's how the brain shell identified itself. Hey, Officer Kirishima, isn't that the name of the guy who was recently kidnapped and then found again?*>

"Do you have a record that proves it was him?"

<*No. That's just the response I got in the short conversation we had.*>

"I see. That's not enough to be sure. Since Masumoto was released unharmed, I doubt the special investigations team will pursue it."

<*True. It is a stolen vehicle, though—we could file a report.*>

"No. This is my case."

<*Huh?*>

"This is my chance to get back into Investigations!"

Officer Kirishima went back to her Minipat. She opened the battered door, climbed inside, and started the engine.

<*You mean you're going to go after the suspects all by yourself?*>

"Yes."

She hit the accelerator. Despite her injuries, she zoomed out of the parking lot.

<*Take me with you!*> I sped after her.

Chapter 4

Together, we darted out of the parking lot. But the car we were chasing was nowhere to be seen. There we were, with no clue as to which way to go.

"Where . . ."

<*Shall we search?*>

"But how?"

<*On the Net.*>

The Net contains a world of pure information that reflects the actual physical world. It consists of a visual display of information gathered from countless data-collection terminals, including GPS and N systems.

This data-based realm is made up of light, values, and symbols.

The Linkline.

Each datum flows to a multitude of data-processing units.

When someone uses a cybercomm, the path their line takes

through the Net is highlighted. When someone makes a credit charge to their deposit card at a bank, you can see the route their money takes. All sorts of information is collected in this terminal: loans from credit companies, account information from banks, and so forth.

The intimate links between the data are what make up this information.

She and I floated in this world of information, with nothing to mark our existence but symbols indicating our location.

Around us, there were all kinds of other symbols, indicating people, shops, signs, public terminals, and so forth.

I eliminated everything but road and vehicle information.

Then I searched the vehicles for the relevant license number.

MNB-LKJ 389.

I scanned the roads.

A hit! R235. Port entrance. Heading toward the East District.

<*I found it!*> I sang.

"Which way are they headed?"

<*They just got onto Route 235 from the Port freeway entrance. They're still within our precinct, but just barely. What should we do?*>

"We go after them, of course. We can still make it!"

Officer Kirishima put her flashing lights on. The shriek of her siren filled the streets. She stepped on the gas. A cloud of white smoke rose up from the Minipat's wheels as it spurted forward, rear end waggling.

<*Hey, wait for me!*>

Hastily, I sped off after her.

Her siren blaring, she threaded past the other cars. Her flashing red lights streamed down the road.

She took full advantage of the agility her compact stature allowed. Angry shouts and honks faded into the distance behind us. We came to a red light but she ignored it, whooshing past the nose of a truck that was coming from one side. Had it hit her, she would have been flattened!

While I was marveling, the side of the truck came right into my path!

<YIKES!>

I hopped over it.

Normally, I can travel a lot faster in these situations, since I would take a direct route instead of sticking to the roads.

For her, it was a matter of getting to the freeway. After that, there wouldn't be any red lights. If she could just get past those lights, she'd be able to really floor it.

I dove into the police traffic terminal and fiddled with the traffic-light control program.

Emergency vehicle PC-113. Maintain open roads.

Now all of the lights on her route would remain green until she was past. I borrowed the system that street cars use to stay on schedule for her benefit.

She would be okay now.

But my work wasn't done. If I didn't do something to stop the car with the brain shell in it, we'd never catch up.

At Section 9, we'd use a Tiltorotor to pursue the vehicle from the sky, but at the time I was working as a Niihama Police Harbor Precinct Tachikoma.

I took over the freeway's traffic congestion regulation system and fiddled with the traffic signs on the road ahead of the fleeing car. To slow things down, I created a fake traffic accident and restricted the vehicles to a single lane.

I wanted to funnel a lot of vehicles into the junctions up ahead of the perps, so I issued instructions on other freeways, creating detours onto our route.

On the Net, the line representing the freeway went from green to yellow—a color-coded system indicating traffic congestion.

Up ahead of them, there was a construction area with a parking lot on the other side. If they escaped into the parking lot, there was a risk that they might switch cars on us. Somehow, we had to get to them before they had the chance.

Their car stopped moving.

I drove up alongside Officer Kirishima.

<Officer Kirishima! I got them stuck in a traffic jam! This is our chance!>

"You caused a traffic jam?"

<Eh-heh,> I chuckled bashfully. *<It was no big deal, really. According to the simulation I ran, if we cut underneath and get onto the freeway from the East Port ramp, two entrances from here, we can intersect with them within three hundred seconds.>*

"Right. Thanks!"

<But Officer . . . how come this is so important to you?>

"I guess it's just in my blood."

<Your blood? You mean your blood plasma?>

"No, I mean that my parents instilled me with a sense of pride."

<Your parents?> I don't have any parents. I guess, in a way, the engineers that built my body and designed the platform for my AI are the parents who gave me life.

She continued, "My father was a detective in the Investigations Division of the Prefectural Police."

<A detective . . . what division does he work for now?>

She paused. "He's dead."

<Did he die in the line of duty?>

"No. It was his day off. He and I went for a drive. There was a traffic accident and he was killed. That was fifteen years ago."

<I'm very sorry for your loss . . . >

"I lost my father and my body in that accident."

<Your body?!>

"I was just eight years old. My entire body aside from my right arm had to be replaced with prosthetics."

I looked at her right hand, which she was using to steer the car.

So that was the only part of her that was human flesh.

"It was really rough. Whenever I saw a police officer, I remembered my father . . . I even lived overseas for a while. I thought that perhaps the police in a foreign country wouldn't dredge up the same memories."

<Why did you join the police force if it was so painful for you?>

She hesitated. "It's hard to explain. I came back to Japan to renew my visa and I planned to dispose of all of my family's belongings here. When I was going through them, I found my father's journal—he'd kept it hidden. My father had a strong sense of justice. He had no tolerance for wrongdoing, and he never gave up. Just before he was killed, he'd been taken off the case of a certain politician's murder. He wrote in his journal that he spent as much time with me as possible to help him take his mind off of it—I guess it made him feel better. Even though they took him off the investigation, he didn't let it go. My father was the only one who didn't believe the politician's son was responsible for his murder. Then we had the accident, and he was killed, and I had to switch to a cybernetic body. As I read his journal, I started to feel ashamed of myself for running away from reality. I went back to school and became a police officer."

<I see. They say that the apple doesn't fall far from the tree. It's a pithy way of expressing the idea that children are always observing their parents' actions and attitudes. They learn through these experiences, so they're influenced by their parents and end up having the same cognitive leanings and tendencies. In a sense, proverbs serve as documentation of various objective observations, don't they?>

"Are you really a robot?"

<Well, technically I am, but my cognitive structures are growing more and more human.>

"I think you and I will make a good team."

<Thank you. Oh! We're almost at the freeway entrance.>

"Roger!"

We both accelerated at once.

The path ahead was wide open.

I bet we raised a few eyebrows among the local residents: A Minipat and an AI tank with the same two-toned paint job jetting down the road at top speed, sirens blaring and lights flashing!

We reached the freeway entrance in approximately 170 seconds and crossed under the gate. To our left, a looping ramp led up to the freeway. The Minipat's tires squealed.

Her tires weren't very thick, so they didn't have good traction.

Officer Kirishima let up on the accelerator a little, sensing her vehicle was at its limit.

<Don't slow down!> I called out to her, edging close to her right side.

I touched the Minipat lightly as I extended one leg toward the concrete wall.

The Minipat's body bulged outward from the centrifugal force as her weight pushed my leg against the wall. I leaned harder against the Minipat and continued up the loop line, driving at an angle. Then the curve slackened and the road straightened. The Minipat regained its equilibrium as we hit the freeway with plenty of speed.

The Minipat blared her siren as we sped up the shoulder of the congested road. I followed behind her. My driving motor was almost at the point of burning out! Never before had I driven at top speed for such a continuous stretch of time. We Tachikomas are tanks, but our design was geared more toward walking, not cruising, so we're not really well suited to high-speed chases.

We would arrive at our target—the car with the brain shell in it—in approximately twenty seconds.

A road-construction fence lined the left side of the road. On the other side, work was being conducted to widen the freeway. The fence stretched down the road as far as the eye could see.

We drove on alongside this fence.

Suddenly, a car began to move in one of the lanes.

The red car had seen us. It pulled out of its lane and began to drive away.

"They're getting away!" Officer Kirishima cried.

<Don't worry! This is all exactly according to my simulation!>

"Your simulation?"

The red car was now speeding along the shoulder. But it could see that the entrance to the nearby service area was crowded with cars, and it was searching for a way to get through.

It found one: the vehicle gate to the freeway expansion work site.

The red car burst dramatically through the fence and into the construction area.

We were hot on its tail.

The floor of the construction zone was covered with thick steel plates, and the rear end of the Minipat skidded wildly as she zoomed after the red car. I don't recommend driving with tires whose surfaces have been burnt slick in a high-speed chase. But the red car was having similar difficulties: while its engine was more powerful than that of the Minipat, it seemed to be having more trouble maintaining control.

Then the inevitable happened.

The red car swerved violently in an attempt to shake its pursuers. Its rear tires spun sideways and the car began to roll like a bowling ball. Officer Kirishima swerved to avoid it, and the Minipat skidded sideways and began to roll, too.

Worst of all, we were almost at the end of the construction area. There was no road up ahead!

Only a fifty-meter sheer drop—straight into the ocean.

Human beings can't survive that kind of fall, even if they have cybernetic bodies. Cyborgs don't float in the ocean.

That goes for me, too.

<WATCH OUT!>

Even so, I wanted desperately to save her. In a complete panic, I sped to her rescue.

But my driving motors had reached their limit.

The motor in one of my front legs went out, and its wheel locked up. Suddenly, everything was spinning!

Then my emergency brake took effect, and my entire body was launched forward.

<AIIIIIEEEEEE!!>

I began to roll. Out of the corner of my eye, I could see the red car tumble into the fence. Both its front and rear windshields were dashed to pieces. The trunk swung open, its lock unable to withstand the external pressure.

I looked back in her direction. She was still rolling with a lot of force. If I didn't do something, it was clear that she would go over the edge.

Even at top speed, I wouldn't be able to reach her in time. I'd have a 100 percent success rate if I my goal was simply to save myself, but if I tried to rescue her, my chances would fall to below 25 percent.

And yet—

I had to save her.

The conviction saturated my neurochips. I don't know if it was fate, or just my programming.

My assignment was to record my activities with the police and bring that record back to Public Safety Section 9.

It was my duty. I *had* to return to Section 9.

And yet—

My body moved faster than my thoughts.

I could see her.

From my rear pod, I launched my liquid wires at her. As they sprayed into the air, the oxygen solidified them, turning them into ultra-flexible, super-strong cables. They snared the body of the rolling Minipat.

Her weight pulled me forward.

I was dragged along the iron sheets, shaving down my exterior and sending off a shower of sparks.

I couldn't stop.

I still couldn't stop!

Stop!

STOP!

Her body reached the edge of the cliff and her kinetic energy changed direction from horizontal to vertical.

Gravity reigned.

I pulled my skidding body upright and planted my flailing limbs on the ground.

<Come on, engines!>

I knew that I was short the engine power of one leg. But this was my last recourse.

I turned my back toward the cliff and drove against the force of gravity.

My motors grew hotter and hotter.

My reinforced rubber tires made skid marks on the iron sheets, leaving a testament to my tooth-and-nail struggle against the odds.

Seven more meters.

I used my leg with the burnt-out engine to kick the ground. I kicked and kicked, trying to push myself in the opposite direction from the one in which I was being pulled. The wheel was soon smashed to pieces. Even as my leg began to disintegrate, I continued to struggle against gravity.

I was beginning to decelerate.

Now it was just a matter of whether I could come to a stop in time.

Four more meters.

Stop!

That was the only thought in my mind.

Just when I felt the ocean rearing up behind me, my kinetic energy reached zero.

The blue sky.

That was the image recorded by the camera in my eyeballs. Soft white clouds floated gently above me. *So this is what it feels like to be at peace,* I thought.

Gingerly, I looked down.

There were less than three millimeters left between me and the edge of the cliff.

Down below, at the end of my liquid wires, the Minipat hung, just a whisker from the ocean's surface.

We were saved!

Two minutes later, I had reeled in my wires and hauled her back up.

The two men who had been driving the red car had died in the crash and their craniums had been crushed by the impact. With their brain shells smashed, it was too late to extract any data to learn who they'd been working for.

We couldn't find the freight from the trunk, either—maybe it fell into the ocean.

Officer Kirishima gazed in astonishment at her tattered partner.

She was looking pretty tattered herself.

If she'd had a flesh-and-blood body or a regular cyberbody, she probably would have been dead. But I knew that her body had undergone special processing.

Even still, various parts of it were damaged, and she was clutching her right arm. It was the only non-cybernetic body part she had left.

<Are you okay?>

"Yes. But I don't think my arm is."

Her face was screwed up in pain.

When I'd rescued her, her steering arm had been crushed by the vehicle's door, and the bone was shattered. Her nerves seemed to have been severed, too, and she couldn't even move her fingers.

"I guess I'll have to get a prosthetic arm now, too."

<Then you'll be as good as new!>

Officer Kirishima shook her head.

"This arm was the only flesh-and-blood part I had left. It was my last human part."

All she had to do was replace the arm, and her body would be intact again, with no detriment to her daily affairs. I couldn't understand why she was getting all sentimental about it.

I guess that's the difference between human beings and robots.

Officer Kirishima gazed out at the ocean for a spell, then looked at me.

"The next time we meet, I suppose my entire body will be mechanical, just like a Tachikoma." She smiled.

It was the last time I ever saw her smile.

But from what I could tell, it was an expression of sadness more than any other emotion.

"Tachikoma? What happened to the brain shell?"

<I think it fell into the ocean.>

"Oh."

She looked at me. "Hey, Tachikoma . . . "

<Yes?>

"Thank you. I think I'll be okay with my cyberbody now, thanks to you."

<There's no need to thank me. This sort of thing is our daily fare at Public Safety Section 9.>

"Do you belong to Public Safety Section 9?"

<Er, no. Uh, I belong to the prefectural police. Um, is something wrong?>

Officer Kirishima shook her head. She'd been about to say

something, but she was interrupted by the siren of a string of police cars that had noticed the accident and had come barreling in.

Red lights flashing, the three vehicles pulled into the entrance to the construction site from the freeway.

<There's your ride.>

"Yes. I supposed it's time . . ."

The shriek of the sirens drowned out the end of her sentence.

Those were the last words that passed between us.

<You mean you'll never see her again?>

<After that incident, the Minipat and I were hauled off by a tow truck. Officer Kirishima rode back in one of the police cars. After I was done being repaired, I was sent back here to Section 9 and . . . >

<Sent back to Section 9 and?>

<The truth is, I do hope to see her again.>

<That's a pretty bold statement!>

<You aren't scheming to run away, are you?>

<I'm not scheming to do anything. I have permission from the major already.>

<What? No faaaaair!>

<Well, come on! I have to pay a final visit to the Harbor Precinct to thank them for having me. The major says so, too.>

Chapter 5

This is the first time I've been to the Harbor Precinct in a week.

Finally, I will see her again.

Perhaps it is this thought that leads me to stop and buy a bouquet of flowers on the way. I tell them to send the bill to Daisuke Aramaki. The bouquet is full of little white flowers, but I don't know what they are called.

What is happening in my mind?

She's become the dominant item in my cognitive priority system. Also, I have selfish urges to keep my thoughts of her to myself, and not to share them with the other Tachikomas when we synchronize our memories.

I am happy. I don't know if it is because I am acting alone, but this new thought pattern taking shape in my neurochips makes my spirits soar!

When I arrive at the Harbor Precinct, I head straight for the garage. Inside, everything is just as it was one week ago, with police inspectors checking the black-and-white police vehicles.

But she is nowhere to be seen.

A policewoman notices me and draws near.

"Hey, aren't you the robot from the Prefectural Police?"

I've never seen her before.

<*Excuse me . . . can you tell me where Officer Kirishima is?*> I inquire.

"Officer Kirishima? I think she was the officer I was sent here to replace . . . "

<*You're her replacement?*>

"Yes. I was assigned here just three days ago. The transfer was very sudden, so I'm still just getting a handle on things."

<*Oh, I see . . .* >

"Hold on just a minute. I'll ask for you, okay?"

The policewoman returns to the group.

She's not here.

Somehow, my cognitive processes feel less pleasant now.

The policewoman returns.

"Apparently, Officer Kirishima left the force three days ago."

<*She left the force?*>

"Yes. It was a surprise to me, too—apparently, she went after a stolen vehicle a week ago and got in a major accident. Both suspects in the stolen car were killed in the accident, and the Minipat she was driving was completely totaled. There was a bit of a fuss because she was acting independently, without instructions from above. In the end, she stepped down out of a sense of responsibility."

<*. . . Oh.*>

It feels like my thoughts are completely frozen.

"Are you called 'Tachikoma'?"

<*Yes, that's me.*>

The policewoman hands me a package.

"Officer Kirishima left this for you."

<*For me?*>

I take the package from her and open it. Inside is Officer Kirishima's father's journal.

When I arrive back at Section 9, the other Tachikomas are having their data synchronized.

In the dimly lit warehouse, I find an empty storage space.

I connect up my battery and turn down my sensory organs.

Sight, hearing, touch, smell. Normally, when I turn these senses off, it allows my entity to sink deep down into a sea of thought—a feeling I've experienced many times before. The sea is made up of liquid information. I melt into it, becoming a part of it once again. When a few hours have passed, I hit my start-up switch and return to reality, a new Tachikoma.

But this time, I cannot immerse myself in that ocean.

I feel left behind and alone. Negative thoughts flood my neurochip solution.

"Tachikoma, you're back."

I activate my vision toward the voice that is addressing me.

The major is standing just in front of me.

<*What can I do for you, Major?*>

"How long to plan to stay like that?"

<*Stay like what?*>

"That police look. I've called the Red Suits. When they get here, have them return you to normal, okay?"

<*So I guess that means . . .* >

"Yes. You'll resume your regular duties tomorrow. The residual effects of the thought bomb seem to be minimal; from what we've seen, you should be absolutely capable of performing your work here."

<*I see.*>

There is something inside of me I just can't reconcile. It's like some sort of cognitive disruption that stems from Officer Kirishima's being gone. My stint with the police is over, and so is my relationship with her. But I don't want to erase the memory of the time we'd spent together.

I am pretty sure that my police experiences won't be of any use in my work at Section 9. They'll probably be earmarked for deletion very soon.

But I don't want to forget her.

I guess this is a function of the human phenomenon called "emotion."

In other words, I have acquired the ability to have feelings.

<*Um, Major? Am I a robot?*>

"Why do you ask?"

<*Uh, well, I was just wondering . . .* >

"Your body is mechanical, but you have sentient qualities. In that sense, you and I share a similar existence. But if there is a difference between us, it's that a human being is born with no specific purpose, whereas a robot has one. That's about it, really."

<*Oh, I see! Then, what would happen to me if I became disengaged from that purpose?*>

Just then, the Red Suits arrive.

"We'll cross that bridge when we come to it," the major says, standing up.

<*Oh . . .*>

"By the way, I understand that Officer Nana Kirishima is no longer with the prefectural police."

<*Yes. I heard about it, too. She left this for me.*>

I hand the major the journal.

"Detective Kirishima's journal?" The Major rifles through a few pages of the journal and gives me a perplexed look. "Tachikoma, Officer Kirishima gave you this?"

<*Yes.*>

"Did you tell her that you were from Public Safety Section 9?"

I hesitate. <*Yes. I'm afraid my language function slipped . . .*>

"I see." She walks away without saying anything more.

I watch as she exits the warehouse.

The Red Suits quickly reconfigure my body for Section 9 work.

They remove my two-toned paint job and peel off my Niihama Police decal. They detach the revolving light from my head and replace my antennae, dismantle the speaker installed in my mouth, and reattach my grenade launchers.

In less than an hour, I am restored to my old blue self.

I am no longer just a machine. Now, I am a weapon again.

The Red Suits leave and I am alone again.

The external attributes that made me unique are gone; nothing remains to distinguish me from my peers.

Soon, the memories stored in my neurochips will travel through a cable to create a backup record of my activities, and the synchronization process will begin.

My memories will sink deep into a sea of information. My experiences will be condensed into a solitary record. When memories are converted into a record, they become nothing but data. When I next awake, even if I replay that record, that cognitive disturbance will be gone.

When that happens, I will truly be a Public Safety Section 9 Tachikoma once more.

If I ever see Officer Kirishima again, will I be able to remember my feelings for her?

I don't want to forget.

That's why, until the moment that moment that my memory becomes a record, I will think about her as I fall asleep.

the original episodes of STAND ALONE COMPLEX

#04

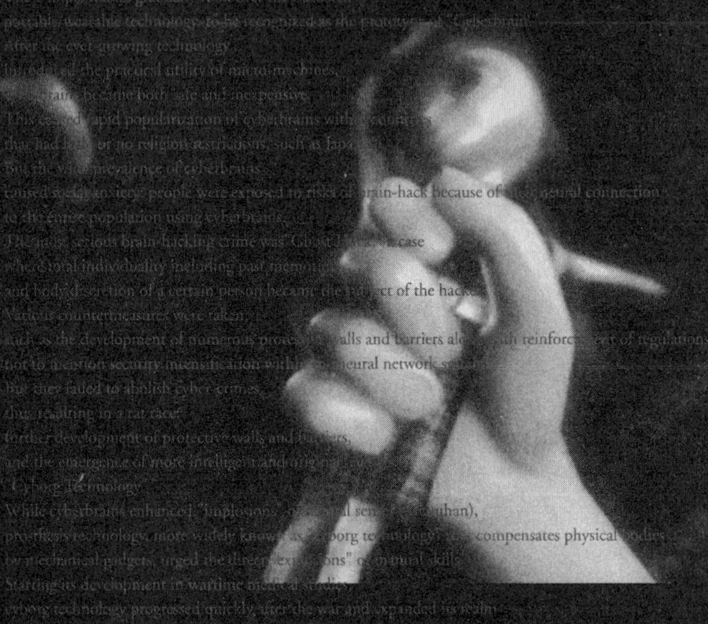

凍える機械

REVENGE OF THE COLD MACHINES

Chapter 1

Morning in the Refugee Residential Zone began with the smell of the food service wafting through the park. A long line of refugees was waiting to be served, each with a plastic or aluminum bowl in hand.

Unfortunately, the rain the night before had turned the turf into a quagmire. A one-legged man on crutches was struggling through the mud, trying to get to the food line.

The man wore a hand-knit hat pulled low over his forehead, almost hiding his dark, cloudy eyes. The fine lines around his eyes added to the aura of age that accompanied him.

His walk was halting, as if he wasn't yet used to the crutches. His clothing was dirty but well-tailored, suggesting that his previous life had been a comfortable one.

Probably a fence-climber.

Fence-climbers were considered a nuisance by the original refugees residing in the Refugee Residential Zones. It was a term used for homeless people who had found their way into the Zones from other areas. Most of the refugees residing here were "disaster exiles": they had been dispossessed of their homelands by the war or other external circumstances. The fence-climbers, on the other hand, were "societal exiles"; people who had dropped out of their everyday lives for various reasons. For some it was financial—they had gone bankrupt and were unable to get back on their feet. Others had committed crimes and were on the lam. Usually, the societal exiles ended up here due to their own decisions.

But for the most part, nobody in the Zones made a point of asking each other about their prior lives. The disaster exiles and the fence-climbers all had one thing in common: both groups didn't relish discussing their past. This was true of almost all of the people gathered today in the park to line up for food.

Step by step, the elderly man tottered forward through the mud on his crutches. Just then, a crutch stuck in the mud and slipped out from under him. Deprived of his support, the man began to teeter over sideways. But before he hit the ground, a pair of arms caught him from behind and held him up.

"Are you okay, mister?"

The old man turned. A young man was gazing down at him.

"Thank you," the old man said.

The young man helped the older man over to a park bench under a zelkova tree. It was in a quiet spot, slightly removed from the line of people. Once the old man was seated, the young man lined up again and returned to the bench carrying two bowls. He gave one of them to the old man.

It was full of hot rice porridge.

The young man sat down next to the old man on the bench and began to wolf down his food. He held the bowl up to his face and used his small spoon to shovel it into his mouth. There wasn't much porridge to begin with, and the young man devoured it so fiercely that he looked like he might eat the bowl, too. When the porridge was gone, he used his finger to get every last drop that stuck to the sides of the bowl.

The way he ate bespoke a vigorous survival instinct.

"Delicious!" he said when he was finished, lowering the bowl from his face.

The old man knew what the porridge was like. It was plain white rice porridge, completely devoid of seasoning or flavor. On occasion, it might contain tiny shreds of an unidentifiable meat of some kind. In all honesty, there was nothing delicious about it at all.

This young man obviously had something to live for.

He reminded the elderly man of his own youth.

The old man offered his own bowl to the young man. The young man took it eagerly.

"Are you sure?"

"Yes."

"But mister, you won't stay alive if you don't eat when you have the chance."

"Don't worry. I had a real feast just the other day." He gazed down at his missing limb. "Had to sell my leg, though."

That was three days ago. The old man had sold his own cybernetic leg to buy food.

He had been living like this for a month now. The old man could tolerate any discomfort when it came to clothing and shelter. But food was another matter.

At first, the food service porridge had been an interesting novelty. But the days wore on, and when a week had gone by, the old man had begun to feel like some kind of farm animal—a beast casually kept alive by the food dumped in its trough.

He craved the taste of fresh-baked bread.

He could almost smell the aroma of the burning juices dripping off of a piece of meat. His mouth yearned to taste the sweetness of melted fat.

"Before I came here, I was the boss of hundreds, you know," he told the young man. "I started a little cybernetic parts business with three friends, right when the fighting was really getting going overseas and domestic industries were all fired up from the wartime special demand. I didn't know a thing about the engineering side, but I knew how to talk to people and how to use my head. That was my role. One of the engineers was really talented, and he managed to patent a hit product. We sold it under the motto of 'light, affordable, and strong.'"

The old man scanned the line of refugees waiting for food. A number of them had cybernetic parts.

"A certain percentage of the refugees here probably owe their parts to our outfit. Business was booming, and we decided to provide prosthetics to refugees at no cost as a sort of public service. We'd made our fortune thanks to the special demand that the war created, so for us it was a way to repay our dues—though I suppose it sounds crude to put it in those terms."

The old man rolled up his sleeve.

When he looked closely, the young man noticed a discreet slit in the man's skin. Other than that, the old man's body was identical to that of a regular flesh-and-blood one.

"I decided voluntarily to replace both of my arms and legs with prosthetics. I wanted to become a billboard for our products. All I needed to do my job were my brain and my mouth. I knew that I couldn't persuade other people to use the parts we made unless I'd tried them myself. That was why I did it."

He looked at the young man.

"You don't seem to have any cybernetic parts," he remarked.

"You're right. I'm impressed that you can tell."

"Cybernetic technology has come a long way, but it's still quite difficult to reproduce the minute nuances of natural human movements. If you know what you're looking for, you can tell the difference."

"I didn't know that."

"These eyes of mine have observed the cybernetics industry for more than twenty years now. The role of the technology has changed over the years. In the beginning, its purpose was purely to replace lost body parts needed to sustain people in their everyday lives."

The old man extended a hand and formed the hand signs for rock, paper, and scissors.

"It took years just to perfect the simple act of sending signals from the brain to an artificial hand to play rock-paper-scissors. But nowadays, most users are looking for features and design, beauty and strength. People acquire prosthetics as a sort of cosmetic surgery. Manufacturers, too, have come to promote their products based on such features. But our company obstinately continued to build cybernetic parts designed to serve as an extension of the body for people who genuinely needed them. "

The old man's shoulders slumped.

" . . . But that's all over now."

"Why's that?"

"We were taken over."

"Taken over?"

"A close affiliate of ours took us for everything we were worth. I have absolutely nothing left." The old man stared at his own hands. "I lost everything. My home, my friends, even my family. All I have left are my cybernetics."

"Wow."

"But you know, I just can't seem to put that life behind me. The other day, I sold my leg, I wanted so badly to eat a tasty meal." He rubbed his remaining leg. "But I've bored you with my story for long enough. It's a pleasure to meet a young person who hasn't lost hope in life."

"The pleasure is all mine, Mr. Toyoda."

The old man's eyes widened.

"How do you know my name?"

The young man pulled an I.D. badge out of his breast pocket.

The sparse print read:

Public Safety Section 9: Togusa

"Public Safety?"

"I began to search for you when I learned that a cyberlimb with your serial number had surfaced on the black market. When you told me your story, I knew it had to be you."

"I have nothing to say to Public Safety! I was a fool to have trusted you!"

Mr. Toyoda stood up, his missing leg causing him to sway dangerously. Togusa reached out to help him, but the old man brushed his hand away.

"Don't touch me! You Public Safety people have put me through enough as it is!"

"I assume you're referring to the suicide bombing fifteen years ago, wherein a large quantity of Toyoda Chemical products were employed."

"That's right. We were investigated for a company-wide conspiracy against the administration!"

"I'd like to ask you to come with me. I'll provide you with food and a warm bed."

"Idiot! I'd sooner die out here in the rain than go anywhere with the likes of you!"

"If that's what you want, I won't stand in your way. But I'd like to ask you a few questions about one of the co-founders of your company, a Mr. Masumoto."

The old man's combativeness melted away.

"Masumoto? You mean Kin'ichi Masumoto?"

"You'll come with me, then?"

Togusa grasped the old man's hand.

Mr. Toyoda didn't resist.

Togusa sent a cybercomm to Kusanagi. "I've taken custody of Mr. Toyoda, Major."

Chapter 2

Ten days had passed since executive director of Toyoda Chemical Kin'ichi Masumoto had returned home after being kidnapped.

There was some concern among the special investigations unit that the incident might develop into a serial extortion case, with numerous related corporations targeted. But as no demands were forthcoming from the perpetrators, the investigators had to consider the possibility that the crime had been motivated by a personal grudge against Mr. Masumoto, who had also served as the firm's business negotiations manager. For now, they were pursuing the case from both angles.

But because Mr. Masumoto had no memory of his own kidnapping and clues to the kidnappers' identities were scant, the police investigation had run aground.

Meanwhile, based on a Tachikoma's discovery of what had seemed to be Mr. Masumoto's brain shell, Public Safety Section

9 was beginning to sense that this case might be far more insidious than it seemed, and its members had begun to keep tabs on the movements of both the Toyoda Chemical corporation and the prefectural police.

In an attempt to answer these questions, the members of Section 9 were gathered in the strategy room, reporting their findings to Chief Aramaki.

"Ishikawa. What's the word on Toyoda Chemical's communications log?"

"I've combed through everything but the specialized circuit for internal communications between the company's affiliates. In their external communications logs, there are 2802 items that relate to the kidnapping incident. They're all chiefly concerned with answering inquiries confirming the facts of the case. I didn't find anything that resembled demands or threats on the part of the kidnappers."

"What about at Masumoto's home?"

"Same deal. I obtained the communications records surrounding the forty-eight hour period when Masumoto was missing, but there was nothing resembling a threat."

Aramaki turned to Paz.

"What did you find at the bank?"

"No suspicious activity. His account showed no evidence of any unusually large deposits or withdrawals."

Aramaki folded his arms and cradled his chin in one hand.

"Then the kidnappers' goal was to get their hands on Kin'ichi Masumoto himself."

"But why?" Batou cut in.

"That's what we find out next. The brain shell the Tachikoma discovered that was identified as Masumoto's should hold the key."

"The one that fell into the ocean? Don't you think it's fish food by now?"

"The major's already gone to retrieve it," Ishikawa told him. "She left as soon as the Tachikoma reported back from the prefectural police. But the tide is swift in that area, so she may or may not be able to find it . . . "

Just then, the door opened and Kusanagi entered the strategy room.

"Speak of the devil," Batou remarked.

"Who, me?"

"Yeah, we were just speculating as to how long your current boyfriend will last."

"Oh, really? I'll let my next boyfriend know you're concerned." She gave Batou an evil look.

"Major. Did you recover the brain shell?" Aramaki asked her.

"I managed it somehow."

"Good. When can we expect the results of the analysis?"

"With a super rush job, seventy-two hours. It's been inundated with salt water, so it has to be desalinated before the process can begin. There's also a chance that the brain has been damaged by spending so much time underwater."

"I see."

"What about Mr. Karnov Toyoda? Was Togusa able to get any information out of him?"

Togusa rose to his feet. "Yes. Kin'ichi Masumoto was one of the founding members that started up Toyoda Chemical with Mr. Toyoda. His background is in engineering."

"That corresponds with the information that's publicly available from Toyoda Chemical," Batou commented. "The three founding members were former chairman Karnov Toyoda, age seventy-two, current chairman Hiroshi Nakajima, age sixty-eight, and executive director Kin'ichi Masumoto, age forty-four, right? But isn't that a bit odd that Masumoto is so much younger than the other two?"

"It seems that Masumoto's father was close friends with Toyoda. Kin'ichi Masumoto was a passionate researcher but hadn't landed a job yet, so Toyoda took him on when he started up his company."

"Just out of the kindness of his heart, huh?" Batou said.

"Yeah. Even though he was shouldering a sudden burden, Toyoda says he was very happy to have Masumoto on board. But as luck would have it, Masumoto turned out to be the goose that laid the golden egg. Back when Toyoda Chemical was still called Toyoda Cybernetics, Masumoto pioneered a technology that dramatically improved the speed with which cybernetic parts reacted to neuro-signals. That patent really strengthened the company, and their profits soared. Two years later, when the president changed their name to Toyoda Chemical, they'd become a cornerstone of the international cybernetics industry, on par with corporations like Poseidon Industry and Megatech Body. It's safe to say that almost all of the cybernetic products manufactured today use the technology they patented."

"I guess that goes for our parts, too," the major said, looking down at her own body.

"As it turned out, there was some intrigue over the patent. Karnov Toyoda wanted to leave the cybernetic technology Masumoto developed unpatented. It was his hope that by keeping it in the public domain, they would stimulate further innovation in the industry. But Masumoto wanted the patent. Apparently, he went ahead with the application process without Toyoda's knowledge."

"So Masumoto wanted the patent for his own personal gain?"

"Actually, he took out the patent in Toyoda Chemical's name, not in his own."

Batou leaned back in his chair. "What a devoted employee! A dying breed!" he scoffed.

"Uh-huh. That was right when a lot of foreign companies were aggressively snooping around for patentable material. If someone else had stolen their technology and patented it out from under them, it would have been a major blow. It was an astute move on Masumoto's part to make sure that didn't happen."

"How did Toyoda react?" Kusanagi asked.

"He didn't hold a grudge. In fact, he even told Masumoto that he'd done the right thing."

"This Toyoda guy sounds like a softy," Batou said.

"Yeah. That's why his company got taken over by Narashino Technobody."

"Relegated to a fence-climber. I guess if someone buys you out, there's not much you can do."

"As it so happens, it seems it was Masumoto who proposed establishing a technology tie-up with Narashino Technobody."

Aramaki started. "Is that so! I seem to remember that the official information released by Toyoda Chemical stated that Narashino initiated the tie-up."

"I'm telling you what Toyoda himself told me. There's no mistake."

"I see."

Kusanagi turned to Ishikawa. "And there wasn't any external trouble prior to the technical collaboration with Narashino Technobody that put Masumoto in any danger, was there?"

"No individuals or groups have clashed directly with Toyoda Chemical. But there was one incident that caused the company to come under Public Safety's scrutiny."

"When they were investigated for complicity in a cybernetic suicide bombing attack fifteen years ago, right?" Kusanagi recalled. "The crime was perpetrated by a terrorist group affiliated with the Human Liberation Front that called themselves Tropic. If I recall correctly, they were dissatisfied with the then administration for providing public funding to the cybernetics industry."

She was answered by Borma, Section 9's specialist in explosives and bomb disarming. "It was a mass slaughter perpetrated by a bomber with a cybernetic body packed with semtex."

"Why did they use a Toyoda cyberbody?"

"The Toyoda cyberbody had just the right spaces in it, probably because its parts are organized in miniaturized units. Normally, those voids are filled by a shock-absorbing gel matter that minimizes the tiny metallic sounds the unit makes. If you remove the gel and replace it with semtex, you've got the perfect cyborg-bomb without an obvious change in weight. The method got its start in the Middle East."

Indiscriminate terrorist attacks using cyborg-bombs were a major social problem. Suicide attackers with explosives strapped to their person were an age-old terrorist technique, but they could be apprehended through careful garment inspections.

But bombers who carried their weapons inside their bodies were unstoppable. This led to the emergence of cyborg-perpetrated suicide attacks.

Fanatic anti-cybernetics terrorist groups foisted their message on society by themselves acquiring cyberbodies to slip past rigorous security inspections and commit suicide bombings.

Toyoda Chemical's cyberbodies were particularly suited to these attacks, since they were easily converted into cyborg-bombs by removing an insulating gel very similar in texture and weight to the explosive that replaced it. Toyoda cybernetics quickly became a mainstay of terrorist massacres.

Borma shrugged. "Even now, used Toyoda cyberbodies bring a pretty penny on the black market in the Refugee Zones. If we just had to deal with the Human Liberation Front, it wouldn't be so bad. But the recent refugee policies have created a lot of unrest. If cyborg refugees start perpetrating these kinds of attacks, they'll be unstoppable."

"Then we'll just have to strike first to make sure that doesn't happen," Aramaki said. "Check the flow of funds connected to the technology tie-up with Narashino Technobody three years back and find out who Masumoto was associating with back then. We'll start there. Major, I want you to direct the on-site maneuvers."

"What will you be doing, Chief?"

"Me? I'll be looking into Representative Kinoshita's case. There's something about it that's nagging at me."

"Now that you mention it, weren't there illicit donations from Toyoda Chemical mixed up in that incident, too?"

"I'll look into it."

"Roger. Let's go!"

At Kusanagi's command, the members of Section 9 flooded out of the strategy room.

Chapter 3

It had happened approximately four days ago.

The man appeared at a bar at the very northern edge of the city.

The place was a real dive. It had a counter and no tables, and was so small that there was only seating for five customers.

"Beer," the man said tersely upon entering the room.

When a can was set in front of him, he poured it into the stein himself. White foam covered the bottom of the glass and rose, lifted by the sparkling amber liquid that filled the cup.

When the crown of foam reached the rim of the glass, he stopped tilting the glass.

The ice-cold beer sat in front of him.

The man stared at it, his mouth watering.

It had been a long, long time since he'd had a beer.

He grasped the stein in both hands and poured it down his throat in a single draught.

It tasted phenomenal.

First, there was the coolness of it as it washed down his throat. Then, the bitter taste that filled his mouth, reminding him of old times.

"I'm home now," the man murmured softly when he had finished his beer.

He'd been in the slammer until just two hours ago.

Back in the war, he'd done a lot of things that he could never tell anyone about. But by acquiring a new cyberbody and face, the man had severed ties with his repugnant past. He'd put the killing fields behind him and had started a family. But no sooner had he achieved this small, humble happiness, than he was called upon to fulfill an old promise. He was asked to commit an assault.

The man had gone out drinking and had gotten into an argument with the Director of Development at a company called Narashino Technobody, and had ended up putting the executive in the hospital. Of course, the drinking was merely a pretense. An acquaintance who knew the man's past had requested that he teach this Director of Development a good lesson.

The acquaintance had once saved the man's life, and he'd felt obligated to comply—at least the favor didn't involve killing anyone.

To pay for his crime, he'd spent the past three years behind bars.

It felt like an unspeakable luxury to now recover the everyday life he had almost forgotten, just by drinking a beer in a squalid little watering hole.

Someone poured a bottle of beer into his empty cup.

The man turned.

"You . . . !"

"Hello, Yō. Long time no see."

The man's name was Tegan Yō. Or at least, that had been his name back on the battlefield.

Yō stared at the man.

"Congratulations on your release."

"Who are you?" Yō had never seen him before.

"Oh, of course—it's only natural that you don't recognize me. I have a job for you."

"A job?"

"To be more precise, I want to see your alter ego. The Tegan Yō 'Twins.'"

The devil was tempting him.

"I have your old face and a military cyberbody ready for you."

"I've put all that behind me."

"But, Yō . . . you have a score to settle with Toyoda Chemical, too, don't you?"

When he heard these words, something stirred inside of Yō. "We're talking about Toyoda Chemical, are we? I'm in." An evil grin spread across his face.

Chapter 4

It was fifteen years ago that Toyoda Cybernetics had purchased a lot in a destroyed section of the city to build its first factory. Clearing away the rubble as they went, they'd expanded their facilities, erecting a skyscraper on their compound seven years ago.

That was right around the time they'd changed their name from the Toyoda Cybernetics Factory to Toyoda Chemical.

A foreign luxury sedan pulled up in front of the main entrance of the Toyoda Chemical building. The driver held the door open as Executive Director Kin'ichi Masumoto stepped out. He wore his graying hair slicked straight back, and his expression was grim as he stepped into the building.

Batou was watching through a telescopic device from an apartment building a little ways away. The device interfaced directly with his cyberbrain, allowing him to enlarge a portion of his field of vision.

"I can count the white hairs on the old bastard's head," he

remarked to Saito, who was set up next to him, peering through the scope of his rifle.

"If you can confirm his identity by counting his white hairs, knock yourself out." The response was icy, but it was definitely typical of Saito's personality. "Notice anything else, Batou?"

"Yeah. That car there was parked in another spot yesterday for just seventeen minutes. It's green today, yesterday it was red. They forgot to change the license plates, though."

The car he was referring to was parked in a spot at a distance from the front doors, but with a view of the entrance.

"Prefectural police?"

"Nah. If it were the cops they'd be undercover, with refurbished plates. The vehicle is a run-of-the-mill economy model. If I recall, it was the top seller two years ago. Right about now there are probably a ton of them available second hand from folks who're upgrading. We've probably got ourselves some kind of ex-intelligence agent here."

"I'm going to go get a look at his face." Saito started for the door.

"You're a glutton for punishment, you know that?"

But the door closed behind Saito before all of Batou's words reached him.

Not many people passed by the street in front of Toyoda Chemical.

Saito stepped out onto a commercial avenue with more foot traffic and flagged down a car with a large, luminous TAXI sign on its roof.

He noticed that the cab driver glanced at his SOS button when he saw Saito climb into the back seat. If he hit the button, the electric sign on the roof would change to read SOS, alerting the outside world that the driver was experiencing trouble.

It was the same every time Saito boarded a taxi.

Saito knew he had a scary face. But compared to some of Section 9's members, like Batou, Paz, or Borma, he looked fairly innocuous.

He wore a black shirt unbuttoned to expose a large expanse of chest, adorned with a heavy gold necklace.

"I want you to drive past Toyoda Chemical and then bring me back here," Saito told the driver in a low voice.

The driver hesitated for a moment before responding, "Yes, sir," and pulled out.

Toyoda Chemical was less than a minute's drive away.

If they obeyed the speed limit, it would take them less than 0.2 seconds to pass by the parked car.

The cabbie put on his right turn signal. When they made the turn, they would be on the street in front of Toyoda Chemical. The car with the man in it would be in the opposite lane.

The light at the intersection was red, and the taxi stopped. Through the left window, Saito could see the apartment building where Batou was staked out.

In a seat by the window of a restaurant on the corner, a man looked out casually in the direction of Toyoda Chemical. His ashtray was piled high with cigarette butts. Probably a prefectural police special investigator.

The light turned green and the taxi turned right.

As the scenery streamed by, Saito spotted the green car parked on the other side of the street.

There was someone inside.

The taxi drove past.

Saito got a glimpse into the car through its front windshield with his peripheral vision. He didn't want to arouse suspicion by staring straight into the car. Even by sliding over into the driver's side of the back seat to get a better view, he might call attention to himself.

The moment was brief, but it sufficed.

The taxi turned right at the corner and returned to the commercial avenue to drop Saito off.

The sharpshooter cybercommed Batou. "Saito speaking."

<How was it? Did you identify our peeping tom?>

"Yeah. It's Tegan Yō. I ran into him a number of times back in the killing fields."

<A mercenary, huh? I haven't heard his name much.>

"He's not extraordinarily talented. But he's the kind who can be counted on to carry out his obligations. Strong willed—the type who never talks under torture."

<What's he want with Toyoda? An engineering job?>

"Spare me the lame jokes."

<Okay, okay. Reporting back to Section 9.>

"Roger. I'll be on my way in a moment. Do you need smokes?"

<Definitely. Sounds like we'll need to calm our nerves.>

After Batou's last response, Saito headed toward a cigarette shop.

Chapter 5

When Narashino Technobody had merged with Toyoda Chemical three years back, the former's Director of Development George Narashino had left the company and gone to work for Megatech Body.

Normally, companies made their best efforts to retain their engineers for life, but Narashino was one of the employees who had opposed the merger.

As the son of the company's founder, Narashino was expected to succeed his father as president and CEO. But after his father's sudden death, no sooner had Narashino become president than the board of directors had voted to approve the technological tie-up with Toyoda Chemical.

Narashino hadn't been present during the decision-making process.

It was an act of rebellion based on the board's determination to streamline the company completely, ridding it of its family-business character. Toyoda Chemical was ranked third in Japan and was expected to develop an overseas presence; Narashino Technobody was ranked seventh domestically. The merger would allow them to leapfrog over Poseidon Industry and Megatech Body and become number one in the industry, with more than forty percent of the cybernetics market share. There was no reason for either corporation to oppose the union.

If not for the merger, Narashino would have led a carefree life as president and CEO. But now, as a rank-and-file corporate employee, he had to sweat every day over his performance at work.

Right now, two Niihama prefectural police detectives stood in front of Narashino. They said they wanted to talk with him about the recent abduction of Toyoda Chemical's Masumoto.

"I want an explanation as to why I'm being questioned!" Narashino shouted at the two men, banging his fists on his desk.

The coffee cups on the table jumped.

Narashino was new at this firm, and any sort of scandal could be fatal to his career. He couldn't afford to have anything taint his reputation at this stage. It could hurt him deeply to be the object of a police investigation.

"Mr. Narashino, you're not a suspect. We're just trying to gather information on whether or not there was anyone with a score to settle against Mr. Masumoto."

"Then make an appointment! I can't just have a pair of detectives showing up suddenly in my office!"

"Yes, sir. We'll make an appointment next time. But time is at a premium, so please cooperate with us just this once. This might be connected to something bigger . . . do you remember the Laughing Man incident of six years ago?"

"The Laughing Man incident . . . "

Narashino searched his memory. Now that they mentioned it, the recent assassination attempt on the Superintendent of the Metropolitan Police had caused quite the disturbance, and the name "Laughing Man" had been bandied about here and there.

One of the detectives, the younger one, looked straight into Narashino's eyes.

"In the Laughing Man incident, six micromachine manufacturers were subjected to corporate extortion plots, including Serano Genomics. The whole thing started when someone kidnapped Serano Genomics's CEO. This case, too, began with an abduction, so there may be some sort of connection. That's why we're gathering information from the entire cybernetics industry. We want to know if there have been any threats, any bad blood between affiliated companies, that sort of thing."

Narashino struggled with the fear that if he broke the detective's gaze, he would appear suspect.

He hadn't done anything wrong.

True, he had argued with Masumoto over issues related to the merger. But that was three years ago.

When Narashino had decided to leave Narashino Technobody, Masumoto had tried to stop him, praising Narashino's abilities as an engineer. Masumoto himself had a background in engineering.

But three years ago, Narashino hadn't intended to remain an

engineer forever. He'd been contemplating the transition to company president. Thanks to Toyoda Chemical, the position that was rightfully his was now closed to him.

Of course, he had turned Masumoto away.

But Masumoto hadn't given up.

When Masumoto persisted, Narashino would have the receptionist claim he wasn't in. At other times, he responded with outright rudeness.

But so what?

Was his life going to be flushed down the toilet again because of *this*, now?

"Mr. Narashino, I'd like to ask you one more question." This time, the woman detective addressed him. She was a generic-looking full cyborg. Her commercial-model cyberbody appeared to be a Poseidon. "Were you assaulted by a thug three years ago?"

"Oh, that. Now that you mention it, if not for that incident, I'd probably be the president of Narashino Technobody right now."

"What do you mean?"

"It was a bad time to get beat up. I ended up in the hospital for two months with serious injuries. Even though my father had just died, I was unable to attend the board meetings. That was when they decided to go forward with the technological tie-up with Toyoda Chemical."

"I'm sorry, sir."

"I curse my own bad luck, but I don't harbor resentment toward Masumoto. If I wanted to bear a grudge, it would be against those bastards from the former Narashino board of directors who are now sitting pretty in Toyoda Chemical offices."

"I see. That gives us a much clearer picture. If anything out of the ordinary happens, please contact us." The female detective handed him a card.

On it, her name and cell phone number were printed.

Motoko Kusanagi
Investigations Division
Niihama Prefectural Police

As Kusanagi drove back from Megatech Body, Togusa sat in the passenger seat.

"Did you get anything from that?" He asked her.

"Nothing solid, but it's obvious that Narashino's hospitalization three years ago facilitated the merger with Toyoda Chemical," she replied.

"Someone who stood to gain from the merger set it up to keep Narashino out of the way."

"Yes. There can't be too many people who know about this."

"Current Toyoda Chemical CEO Nakajima and the abducted Masumoto?"

"Excellent powers of deduction."

Togusa laughed self-consciously. "I *am* a former police detective."

"The dynamics of the case all revolve around Toyoda Chemical. When the opportunity comes for us to play our cards, we'll be ready."

"The brain shell, right?"

There was a chance that the brain shell a Tachikoma had discovered during a separate assignment might belong to Masumoto. The analysis process was already underway.

If the brain shell in Section 9's custody did belong to Masumoto, who was the person currently working at Toyoda Chemical whom the authorities had identified as Masumoto?

Which one was the true Masumoto? In order to be sure, they would need the help of someone who had known Masumoto for a long time. To that end, Section 9 had sought out Karnov Toyoda, founding member of Toyoda Chemical. For a time, Toyoda's whereabouts had been unknown, but then a piece of his cyberbody had surfaced in the Refugee Zone. This had enabled them to locate Toyoda and plug him for information about Masumoto and Toyoda Chemical.

That was when they had learned about the upheaval surrounding the merger between Toyoda Chemical and Narashino Technobody.

It was safe to say that an attack on George Narashino, former Director of Development at Narashino Technobody, had enabled the merger to go forward.

There was one missing piece that would make everything clear: Masumoto's brain shell. Togusa had a feeling that it harbored everything they needed to know.

"The analysis should be done soon, shouldn't it?"

"Yes. It's been almost seventy-two hours. When I get back to Section 9, I'll initiate a thorough investigation of that brain shell's role in this case."

Chapter 6

Back at the warehouse at Section 9, the Red Suits were almost finished analyzing the brain shell that had been rescued from the bottom of the ocean.

The Red Suits were Section 9's forensic team. They had toiled without sleep or rest to stabilize the cranium's brainwaves and restore its functions.

If the brain had lingered in the ocean for a half-hour longer, it might have been completely pickled by the sea brine, its story lost forever.

Ishikawa observed the brain's waveforms.

"So you're absolutely sure this brain belongs to Masumoto?"

"Absolutely," one of the Red Suits responded impatiently. "There's nothing to suggest that this is a degraded copy and its neural reactions are completely normal. If these are the respons-es of an Artificial Intelligence program, we human beings are piloted by A.I.s."

<*WHAT DID YOU SAY?*>

The crowd of Tachikomas that had gathered around began to all talk at once.

<*Are you trying to pick a fight or something?*>

<*Yeah! There's no reason to compare us to human beings!*>

<*A.I. programs are capable of infinite growth through the acquisition of experiences. In a sense, they're a kind of cognitive perpetual motion machine with ever-increasing possibilities!*>

<*But endless loops are a bummer.*>

<*Good point!*>

<*More importantly, don't you want to get a peek into that brain shell?*>

<*Oooh, I do! I do!*>

One of the Tachikomas extended a connective cable toward the brain, and the other eight followed suit. Their wires snaked toward the brain, each racing to reach it first.

A hand swooped in, gathering up the cables in its grasp.

<*Hey! What're you doing?*>

The fist belonged to Ishikawa. "Do you guys want to get in trouble with the Major for messing with the brain without permission?" he asked them.

<*I guess not . . .*>

<*Yeah. If the major gets mad at us, she might have us dismantled!*>

<*That would suck!*>

<*Or she might inject us with a weird thought control program that causes obsessive cognitive patterns!*>

<*Yikes! That's even worse!*>

En masse, the Tachikomas filed back toward their lair.

<*Mr. Ishikawa, we didn't do anything, so please don't tell the major we tried to look at the brain!*>

"Got it."

<*Promise!*>

"I promise."

<*When human beings make promises, they do a pinky-swear, right?*>

"Where did you pick that up? It's a very primitive practice."

<*Come on, give me your pinky.*>

Ishikawa extended his little finger. "Let's get on with it, then. I've got work to do."

The Tachikoma grasped Ishikawa's pinky in its manipulator and pumped it up and down.

<*Pinky-swear! Pinky-swear! Liars get a thousand whiskers pulled! There!*>

Ishikawa stroked his beard. "Normally it's 'Liars have to swallow a thousand needles,' you know."

<*Yeah, but isn't that physically implausible?*>

<*It might refer to the fish whose Latin name is* Diodon holocanthus. *One of its common names is 'Thousand Needles.'*>

"That's a blowfish, isn't it? Aren't they poisonous?"

<*The Thousand Needles isn't poisonous. It's supposed to be delicious, too. Unfortunately, we have no sense of taste so we'll never be able to enjoy it.*>

"Fine, fine. Now let me get back to work."

<*Yes, sir!*>

Ishikawa rolled up his sleeves and readied the neuro-exploration device. The Red Suits returned to the forensics room; the rest would be left to Ishikawa.

"Let's see, here . . . "

Ishikawa connected the exploration device to the QRS plug in the back of his own neck. This would enable him to observe a physical representation of the persona housed in the brain's memory in his visual field.

He switched the device on.

The brain reacted.

A blurred human figure appeared in Ishikawa's visual field.

Ishikawa addressed the brain. "Are you Mr. Masumoto?"

<W-who . . . a-are . . . you?>

Because the brain's links with its sensory organs had been shut down for a stretch of time, its connections weren't yet completely recovered. Its word formation abilities seemed impaired—perhaps its linguistic field was still unstable.

"We're police officers. We've taken you into custody."

<I'm in cus-to... cus-tom . . . cus-tard . . . >

Custody. Ishikawa sent the word to him conceptually.

<I'm in police custody?>

Masumoto's speech was becoming clearer and clearer.

Ishikawa made a point of calling Masumoto by name as much as possible in order to encourage the brain to recognize its identity.

"That's right, Mr. Masumoto. You're in police custody."

<Custody. Did something . . . happen . . . to me?>

"Don't you remember, Mr. Masumoto?"

<Remember?>

"Mr. Masumoto, what's the last thing you remember?"

<The last thing . . . dark . . . trembling . . . something peering in . . . a robot . . . >

"You're doing great, Mr. Masumoto."

Ishikawa opened a waveform graph of Masumoto's brain activity in a portion of his visual field. He could see the activity levels growing steadily stronger.

<Yes, I was locked up in a dark place . . . I couldn't move . . . my hands . . . or legs.>

"That's right, Mr. Masumoto. Your hands and legs and everything else only exist as pseudo-signals. Right now, you're just a brain shell."

<Just a . . . brain shell?>

"Yes. Do you remember being assaulted, Mr. Masumoto?"

<I was assaulted?>

"Yes. It was right after you'd gone to bed."

< . . . .>

Masumoto seemed to be searching frantically for the thread of memory. His brain waveforms were reacting.

If this was a pseudo-personality, it was an extremely sophisticated program.

<I . . . yes . . . I remember. I was assaulted that night.>

"Can you describe your attackers?"

< . . . Yes. But it's so dark. I want to go somewhere where it's light.>

"Unfortunately, I can't provide that. It may be hard for you to accept, but right now, you're nothing more than a brain shell. You're only being kept alive by a life-support system and a pseudo-sensory device."

<I see now. So that's why my body feels immobilized.>

"Yes. I'll ask you once again. Please tell me everything you remember, starting with the events of that night."

<Very well. That night, my wife and I had just retired for the night . . . >

Kin'ichi Masumoto lived in a three-story home. For the executive director of a first-tier cybernetics maker, it was a fairly humble abode.

That night, lying next to his wife in bed, Masumoto had suddenly experienced difficulty breathing. He had opened his eyes to the sight of two complete strangers standing over him.

"Who . . . "

He couldn't speak. Something was blocking his mouth.

One of the figures spoke. "We're taking you with us. Don't try to resist."

He looked at his wife. One of them held a knife against her throat.

His wife seemed to be awake, but she, too, was gagged. She seemed to have a strip of duct tape covering her mouth. Masumoto probably did, too.

He decided to obey.

There was no use getting killed.

In this type of crisis, it was important not to excite the attackers. He had to initiate a rational dialogue.

He closed his eyes and tried to calm himself. Someone rolled him over, face down. Then he heard a snapping sound at the nape of his neck. His perceptions of the room were cut off.

How much time had gone by?

The next thing he knew, Masumoto was looking at his own image.

Masumoto looked at Masumoto and smiled.

He felt queasy.

The other Masumoto showed him a large mirror.

Masumoto was speechless. He vomited. No—he wanted to vomit, but he couldn't.

He had the sensation of vomiting, but he couldn't actually do it.

The mirror showed him why.

The image reflected back to him was revolting—a tubular camera lens and a brain. Nothing more.

That was when Masumoto understood that his brain shell had been removed from his body and replaced by somebody else's.

Whoever it was could have just killed him. But they seemed to derive some sick satisfaction from showing him what they had done.

He had no ears.

The other Masumoto seemed to be speaking, but he couldn't hear.

The next thing he knew, he was enveloped in darkness again.

<I'm not sure what happened after that,> Masumoto's brain told Ishikawa.

"I see. They cut off your sensory perceptions and put you to sleep. The fact that they kept you alive means that they still had plans for you."

<*Oh.*>

"Any ideas what that might be?"

<*No.*>

"Hmm."

Masumoto had no recollection of the forty-two hours he had been missing. There was no point in discussing it further. The only thing left was to find a way to prove that this was truly Masumoto's brain.

Just as he was contemplating that thought, Kusanagi and Togusa walked in.

"Any progress, Ishikawa?"

"I just have to ask this brain something that will prove it's the real Masumoto."

"Allow me," Kusanagi said. She took the brain exploration device from Ishikawa and connected up. Masumoto's image appeared in her visual field.

"Mr. Masumoto, I'm sorry this is so sudden, but I'd like to ask you a few questions."

<*Questions?*>

"Do you remember the cybernetic technology Toyoda Chemical patented?"

<*Yes,*> Masumoto's brain quivered.

"I understand that when you patented that technology, you did so without the knowledge of Mr. Toyoda. Why?"

<. . . *It was a decision I made so as not to be outdone by foreign*

corporations, for my own future's sake. Mr. Toyoda wanted everything to be open source. But we never would have gotten anywhere that way. We'd have been a tiny, back-street factory forever.>

"But you were an engineer. Why were you concerned about that sort of thing?"

<*Someone was kind enough to advise me. He said that if I applied for a patent now, that it would definitely be granted. And that it would bring me success.*>

"What did that kind person ask for in exchange?"

<*Nothing much . . .* >

"Can't you tell me?"

< . . . . >

"Very well. I can extract it forcibly from your memory, you know."

< *. . . all right. I'll tell you. He wanted me to donate money to the Minister of Health, Labor, and Welfare.*>

"To Minister Tadayama?"

< *. . . Please, don't make me. . .*>

"Your reaction is answer enough. I'm afraid you'll be somewhat inconvenienced until you can get your body back—sweet dreams."

Kusanagi removed the cable, sending Masumoto's brain back to sleep.

"Ishikawa. Gather information on Masumoto and continue the verification process to confirm his identity."

"Roger. Did you get what you needed? We can extract his memory, you know."

"Masumoto is the central figure in this incident, but he's only a pawn. He may serve as a witness to the Toyoda Chemical scandal, but there's still something bigger lurking in the background. In order for us to unearth that information, it'll be handy to keep him in his current state a little longer."

Kusanagi connected her cybercomm circuits to Batou.

"Batou, do you read me?"

Batou was in the apartment with a view of the Toyoda Chemical building.

He was lying down, his cyberbrain still connected to the telescopic device.

"I read you."

<We're fairly certain that this brain shell belongs to the real Masumoto. I'd like you to apprehend Masumoto's person when he emerges from Toyoda Chemical. We need to find out who the imposter is.>

"What, you want me to become a kidnapper now?"

<Exactly. The details of the maneuver are at KN-098784. Report to the indicated position.>

"Roger. I'm on it."

Batou sat up and addressed Saito. "We've got orders from the major. Let's roll."

"She wants us to nail Masumoto, eh?"

Saito picked up his rifle case.

"Do you really need that?" Batou muttered.

"I'm a cautious guy."

"You could've fooled me."

Batou left the room, and Saito followed.

Chapter 7

It was almost midnight. The number of cars on the road had decreased visibly.

Near a freeway entrance up in the mountains, a van was parked with its headlights off on a side street intersecting with the bypass. Inside the vehicle's dark interior, watchful eyes were monitoring the passing cars.

They belonged to Batou and Saito.

Toyoda Chemical's Masumoto passed this spot everyday when he commuted home from the office.

Batou tapped his index finger against the steering wheel.

"Who's tailing Masumoto right now?"

"Paz and Borma," Saito responded from the passenger seat.

Batou used the GPS to open an elevated view of the surrounding roads on the navigation map.

"Where's their position?"

"I'll send it to the navi system."

He read the map coordinates from the maneuver code the

major had given them and projected them onto the Net map along with the requisite information from the GPS.

Several points of light appeared on the map at the given coordinates.

"This is us, at the center of the screen. This one moving up from the bottom of the screen is Paz and Borma's team. They sealed off the freeway after Masumoto passed through. This big space here alongside the freeway is a rest area. That's where Togusa and Ishikawa's team is. They're our backup. And this is our route. See this long tunnel? The major and Tachikomas are at the other end."

"Got it."

Batou looked to the left. He could see headlights approaching.

Three vehicles.

The first and last cars were domestic, mid-sized models. The middle car was a foreign luxury vehicle.

"Probably the first and last cars are special investigators from the prefectural police, and the one in the middle is Masumoto's car."

"Yeah. Wait until they pass us."

"You telling me what to do, sniper?"

"You better believe it, ranger," Saito shot back, just as the three vehicles drove past.

"Here we go." Batou turned the ignition key to start the engine and pulled out quietly, as if they'd just happened to turn out onto the bypass from the side road.

Then he hit the gas.

The engine roared, and the van spurted forward with a burst of torque.

From the outside, it looked like an ordinary van. But underneath, it was actually a Public Safety Section 9 custom-built hot rod.

The van sped through the bypass onto the freeway entrance. Batou downshifted from the top gear into third and gassed it. The van sprang forward—three tons of steel launched forth like a speeding bullet.

He shifted into top gear, and then into overdrive.

Immediately, his field of vision narrowed.

He felt the vibrations of the road through his hands on the steering wheel.

The sound of the road underneath them changed pitch.

The engine's hum, too, became a high-pitched shriek.

When the cars in front of them were less than five hundred meters away, he matched their speed, maintaining the distance between them.

"What are we going to do about these cops?"

Five hundred meters in front of Batou's van, the undercover investigators in the cars on either side of Masumoto's finally noticed that something was afoot.

The detective at the wheel was alerted by a warning beep from his GPS. He glanced at the monitor.

It was indicating a construction zone near the tunnel exit.

The alert hadn't been there when they'd gotten on the freeway.

"Hey, I don't remember hearing about any construction work."

"Slow down so we can see what's going on!" the investigator in the passenger seat directed.

"Okay." The one at the wheel eased off the accelerator.

But the vehicle showed no signs of slowing.

In fact, it was speeding up.

"Hey, I thought I told you to slow down!"

"I can't! The drive system's been taken over!"

The investigator in the passenger seat looked back at the other police vehicle traveling behind them. Its occupants stared out at them through the front windshield with bewildered gazes. Apparently, their vehicle was missbehaving, too.

The steering wheel rotated left and the car decelerated slightly.

The rear vehicle sped up and veered to the right.

Now the two cars flanked Masumoto's on either side, matching its speed.

Batou observed the spectacle from the van five hundred meters behind them.

From the activity of the cars' taillights, he knew instantly what was going on.

"The Major's up to her tricks again. She's cracked the control codes of both of the undercover cop cars."

"Simultaneously? That's one scary lady."

<You don't like scary ladies?>

Saito's eyes widened at the sudden cybercomm from Kusanagi.

"No, ma'am. I didn't say anything."

<Batou. I've taken care of the cops. Make sure Masumoto's car doesn't escape from the rear.>

"Roger."

Batou stepped on the accelerator.

The tail of Masumoto's car grew rapidly closer.

When they were just one hundred meters away, the GPS issued an alert sound.

Saito noticed it. "HEY! Some moron's coming up the exit ramp the wrong way!"

"Up the exit?!"

They were almost upon the freeway exit.

It was flooded with the glare of a pair of white headlights.

"SHIT!"

Trying to dodge the blinding light, he swerved to the right for a brief instant.

It was a lucky move.

The headlights zoomed straight toward them and swooshed past at an incredible speed, knocking off their left side-mirror.

Their combined speed was 300 kph. The brief vacuum that was created drew the two vehicles together, wrenching them free of their drivers' control.

Batou quickly regained charge of the shaking vehicle.

The car that had streaked by them was a French car—a Peugeot with an evil countenance. They swept through its V6 DOHC exhaust as its tires thrummed against the road behind them.

The Peugeot executed a swift spin turn.

Its momentum sent it into three rotations before it reoriented in the correct direction. Then it shot forward, its tires veiled in white smoke.

Batou's van had fallen back slightly relative to Masumoto's car. When Batou faced forward again, preparing to close in on Masumoto, his rear mirror reflected the glare of headlights closing in on them from behind.

"Already?!"

The Peugeot on their tail had been born for the chase. In the blink of an eye, it was driving alongside them.

Its windows were low to the ground.

As Saito tried to get a look inside, the Peugeot's automatic window rolled down and the barrel of an SMG poked out at him from inside.

"Holy shit!"

Frantically, Saito ducked behind the iron paneling of the door.

A high-velocity armor-piercing shell shattered the window where Saito's head had been an instant earlier and lodged itself in the van's roof.

An onslaught of bullets peppered the van.

"Son of a bitch!"

Batou, too, ducked his head as he steered. Forget about watching the road!

Fortunately, the van's doors were reinforced with a specialized composite material that was almost impenetrable, even with armor-piercing bullets. Despite its ordinary exterior, the vehicle was built like a tank.

In the Peugeot's window, the empty SMG magazine clattered to the ground and skittered down the road behind them.

That was when Saito saw the face of the Peugeot's driver.

"It's 'Twins' Tegan Yō, that bastard!"

Yō pulled in front of them and got between Masumoto's car and the van.

"Ha! Prepare to be squashed!" Batou shouted.

He stepped on the gas. The three-ton van closed in on the less-than-one-ton Peugeot. But the Peugeot was more maneuverable, and it dodged the van's attack.

As if to thank them, a barrage of armor-piercing bullets issued forth from the Peugeot, bursting through its rear windshield.

The first shot sent white cracks through the bullet-proofed glass of the van's front windshield, and the next shot shattered it.

"Damn!" Batou muttered.

He glanced towards the passenger seat. Saito was assembling his Sebro rifle.

"Where're you going to shoot?"

"The tires. Match Yō's speed, just for two seconds, will you? I need to wait for a break in his fire."

"That's asking a lot."

Batou started to raise his head, but another high-speed bullet came flying in at him.

"Is there more than one person in there?!"

"Nope. That's just Yō."

"He can maneuver like that while he's driving?"

"He can do two things at once. That's what he does. Back when he was a mercenary, I saw him waste two enemies at the same time, his right and left hands operating independently. It never occurred to me that he could pull this sort of stunt, too."

"He's just using his cyberbrain to drive the car remotely. But to be able to take well-timed shots at a target behind you—that's something else. It's almost like there are two of him."

They were at a loss.

Just then, a cybercomm flashed in.

<*Need a hand there, Big Guy?*>

"Togusa!"

Batou glanced at the GPS. They were rapidly approaching the service area.

"Perfect timing. Do something about this Peugeot between me and Masumoto, will ya?"

<*You got it. Sit tight!*>

The rest area was built on raised ground. As they streaked by, a pair of headlights came barreling down its exit ramp.

It was Togusa and Ishikawa's car.

Togusa swerved to the right, bumping up against the Peugeot.

The much-lighter vehicle was launched sideways, lurching from the impact.

When all he had to do was drive, Yō's cyberbrain was capable of handling two tasks at once. But the unforeseen impact caused him to panic slightly, interrupting his judgment.

Batou and Saito seized their chance.

Batou focused all of his energies on matching the Peugeot's speed, while Saito poked his rifle through the broken front windshield and aimed a single bullet at the Peugeot's rear tire.

The bullet streaked toward its target, driven by the spin from the gun's rifling.

It all happened in a split second.

The Peugeot's tire blew.

The car began to swerve wildly, unable to stay in control at top speed with only three wheels.

Its tail skidded to the right and then the left. Then it plowed straight into the green belt and was launched into the air.

"We did it!"

The Peugeot faded into the distance.

Far behind them, a burst of flame appeared in the sky. Then they heard the explosion.

Batou looked forward again.

They were almost at the tunnel.

Masumoto's car was still flanked by the two undercover police cars.

"Togusa, take the front."

<Roger.>

Togusa's car passed Masumoto's and got ahead of it.

Masumoto's car was forced to slow down.

Batou capped off the rear.

"Got him, Major."

<Roger. Escort him past the tunnel.>

"Hey, you know I'm the master of this stuff!"

There was no response whatsoever from Kusanagi. Dissed!

In the passenger seat, Saito burst into laughter, clutching his stomach.

"It wasn't that funny."

"Pathetic!"

They could see the tunnel's entrance.

The passage was 1,644 meters long.

Togusa's car slowed as it entered the tunnel. Masumoto's car butted up against it and was forced to decelerate as well.

Masumoto stuck his upper body out of his car's sunroof as if in surrender.

He stood up in his car, facing Batou.

"What's he up to now?"

<*He knows we've got him,*> Togusa cybercommed.

"Now we'll get the full story from whoever's running around in Masumoto's cyberbody. Find out what they were scheming."

The yellowish light illuminated Masumoto's face.

The tunnel's lights streamed past over his head.

His face was light, then dark, then light, then dark.

Now they were moving slowly, and all that remained was to find a good stopping place. The exit Kusanagi had mentioned was about eight hundred meters away.

<*Mr. Batou!*> a Tachikoma's voice called.

The Tachikomas that had been waiting with Kusanagi at the exit had come to meet them.

"Here's the welcome wagon!"

<*Way to go, Mr. Batou! You made it look so easy!*>

<*Yeah, we didn't even have a chance to help!*>

"It was nothing. Just takes talent, that's all."

Togusa cut in. "You haven't forgotten how I saved your ass, have you?"

"Please! It's our job to back each other up during operations. Nobody saved anyone's ass."

<*Excellent rationalization!*>

"I'm not rationalizing! Oh, never mind. Our work's almost done."

They would reach the end of the tunnel any minute now.

Or so they all thought.

Just then, an explosion resounded behind them.

Batou glanced at his mirrors. A single headlight was speeding toward them.

"Another one!?"

The shriek of a two-stroke single-cylinder engine grew closer.

That was when Batou saw him. "Yō!"

It was Tegan Yō on a motorcycle.

Apparently, the enormous fireball had only singed his skin.

Yō was riding an off-road motorbike—the kind that folded up to fit in the trunk of a car. It was zeroing in on them at an incredible speed.

Saito readied his Sebro rifle, but the glare of the headlight and the bike's nimble movements made it difficult to aim.

"Shit!"

Saito gnashed his teeth.

The off-roader's headlight swayed from side to side.

Togusa pointed his Mateba. "Freeze!"

"Don't talk, shoot!" Batou shouted, squeezing the trigger of his FN High Power.

A high-speed armor-piercing bullet hit Yō's body.

But his speed never faltered.

Bullets that could pierce a cyberbody and shatter its very core weren't enough to stop Tegan Yō.

The off-roader sped still faster, then disappeared from view.

They scanned the road, trying to see where it had gone.

The off-roader's textured tires gripped the walls of the tunnel. Using centrifugal force, it sped up the round tunnel walls.

In an instant, it was over Masumoto's head.

Batou and Togusa looked up.

As he trained his vision upwards, Batou fired his FN High Power.

The shot pierced Yō's head.

Suddenly, a deafening sound and a burst of light shattered the air.

Whiteness.

Then contrast began to return.

When their vision recovered, the off-roader was nowhere to be seen.

Kusanagi entered the tunnel. "Looks like someone set off an acoustic flash bomb. What happened?" she asked Batou.

Batou stared at the tunnel and the FN High Power in his hand with annoyance. "I plugged that asshole with high-speed armor-piercing bullets and they didn't even faze him!"

He picked up a bullet that was lying on the freeway. It was squashed flat. "Look at this. They bounced right off of him!"

"Never mind that. Where's Masumoto?"

Batou looked at Masumoto's car. He was no longer standing in the sun roof.

"Huh? Where'd he go?"

Her Sebro at the ready, Kusanagi approached the vehicle.

"He's here."

"Wha . . .?"

"Inside the car."

Masumoto was slumped against the car seat.

Batou peered in. "Guess he knew when he was beat!"

"Maybe."

Gingerly, she opened the car door and quickly held the Sebro in Masumoto's face.

"Get out."

Masumoto didn't move.

"Don't tell me . . . "

She holstered her gun and dragged Masumoto out of the car. He showed no resistance.

Batou gazed down at the body.

"What the hell did they pull?"

Kusanagi placed a hand on Masumoto's head and pushed his cranial latch button.

With a sucking sound, the front and back halves of the cranium split open.

"It's gone . . . " Batou murmured.

"Someone snatched the brain shell out when the acoustic flash bomb went off," Kusanagi observed.

They stared down at Masumoto's empty cranium.

Chapter 8

Batou sat alone on a bench in the locker room at Public Safety Section 9.

He stared at the squashed bullet in the palm of his hand.

"What kind of cyberbody is that bastard using, anyway?"

He shifted his gaze to the Custom FN High Power lying at his side.

It was a semi-automatic, originally manufactured by Fabrique Nationale in Belgium. Section 9 had reinforced the rigidity of the entire gun so that it could shoot high-speed armor-piercing bullets.

Batou was sure that all of the shots he had fired had hit their mark.

The armor-piercing shells were low-caliber, but they were powerful enough to penetrate and destroy the very core of a cybernetic body.

The Land Self-Defense Forces did have Sagawa Amored Suits that could deflect such bullets. But the man he'd encountered yesterday was definitely a cyborg.

If the cyborg-criminal element got hold of that sort of technology, they'd be completely immune to the police. If armor-piercing bullets didn't do the trick, no handgun would. They were getting into the realm of artillery.

They would need a military arsenal!

What on earth did Tegan Yō—and the owner of the brain he had absconded with—plan to do with a cyberbody like that?

"Do they want to wage war in the streets?" Batou muttered bitterly.

"That cyberbody really ruffled you, didn't it?"

Batou turned. Kusanagi was standing at the door of the locker room.

"What are you doing in here? This is the men's locker room. No women allowed."

"That doesn't bother me." Kusanagi strode into the room.

"It bothers *me*."

"Oh, does it?" She sat down next to him, unconcerned.

"Apparently, Toyoda Chemical and the Land SDF developed the prototype together," she told him.

"A military cyberbody, eh? No wonder this little pea-shooter didn't faze it." He picked up the FN High Power. "Did Masumoto spill his guts?"

"Don't be crude. He's cooperating with us, that's all."

His cyberbody restored to him, Masumoto had revealed a lot of information about Toyoda Chemical's operations to Aramaki and Kusanagi.

After Toyoda Chemical's merger with Narashino Technobody,

they had diverged from founding member Karnov Toyoda's original philosophy of "Cyberbodies for the People" to a doctrine of "Technology Makes the Body." Rather than creating bodies based on the needs of the customer, they focused on developing products for their own sake and then marketing them to consumers.

When ex-engineer Masumoto took on a central role in the company's management, he'd painted an even more ambitious future for Toyoda Chemical. They would use their technological superiority to appeal to the public.

Collaborating with the military would serve that goal.

Military cyberbodies had to be able to achieve their missions under extreme conditions. It was the ultimate opportunity to take their technological proficiency to a new level, pushing their research to the limit.

"Seven of those military cyberbodies left Toyoda headquarters while the fake Masumoto was there," Kusanagi informed him.

"*Seven*?! So that son-of-a-bitch on the off-roader . . . "

"That was one of them. According to the data we received from Toyoda Chemical, they put special emphasis in increasing the shock-absorbency and impenetrability of the artificial skin. Low-caliber, high-velocity armor-piercing firepower *is* no better than a pea-shooter. Of course, they've jacked up the cyberbody's power output capacity to an unheard-of level, too. The most frightening part is that they've crammed all of that into a cyberbody the same size as a normal human being. Leave it to Toyoda!"

"Just what do these assholes intend to pull with cyberbodies like that?" Batou wanted to know.

Just then, a cybercomm from Ishikawa flashed in.

<Major, Karnov Toyoda is on the move.>

Kusanagi's eyes narrowed. "Toyoda, huh?"

Chapter 9

The compound that bustled with activity during the day was quiet at this hour.

It was one A.M.

On the sixty-fifth floor of Toyoda Chemical headquarters, at an elevation of three hundred meters, a light glowed in the window of the CEO's office.

Karnov Toyoda was paying a visit to his former workplace.

With his crutch and his dirty clothes, he stood out in sharp contrast against the elegantly appointed room. In his absence, various pieces of furniture had been acquired, and the carpet's pile was thicker than before.

Toyoda had always spent more time walking the factory floor, wearing coveralls, so he didn't harbor much nostalgia for this office.

"I see you've redone everything."

"How long has it been, Mr. Toyoda—two years? You've changed

quite a bit yourself."

Toyoda looked at Nakajima, who was seated in the CEO's chair.

"You look pretty comfortable in that chair. But what do you intend to do about you-know-what?"

"I'm afraid I don't know what you're talking about."

"You think I don't know, don't you? I'm talking about the Ground SDF cyberbodies. Toyoda Chemical didn't come this far in developing cybernetic technologies to build that sort of thing."

"How many times do I have to tell that Masumoto—that project was supposed to be top secret!"

"Who put Masumoto up to the merger? I know he wasn't the kind of man to pursue something like this on his own."

"Masumoto? I know he was pretty tight with that young fellow over at Mr. Kinoshita's."

"Representative Kinoshita's secretary, huh? His name was Sakazaki, if I'm not mistaken?"

"Yes. Wasn't he the son of the ex-Minister of Health, Labor, and Welfare?"

Toyoda glared at Nakajima.

"Minister Tadayama, who fell from grace when word got out of the illicit donations he was collecting . . . you and Kinoshita cooked that scandal up together, didn't you?"

"Can you prove that?"

"You think I was born yesterday, don't you, Nakajima?"

The air in the room was tense.

"Mr. Toyoda, is this what you called me in to discuss at this ungodly hour?"

A look of mild surprise crossed Toyoda's face.

"What do you mean? You're the one who summoned me!"

There was a moment of silence.

"What the hell is going on?" they both wondered aloud.

That was when they heard the explosion.

Both men instantly looked out the window toward the front of the building. Perhaps some sort of gas explosion had taken place somewhere in the city. Or maybe it was one of the terrorist attacks that had been cropping up more and more frequently.

Sure enough, a column of black smoke was rising up into the sky.

But it was emanating from right below them.

The trembling floor told the story with eloquence.

"It came from downstairs!" Nakajima shouted.

The explosion had taken place on the first floor of Toyoda Chemical headquarters.

It wasn't big enough to bring down the entire building, but the entire entrance hall was reduced to rubble. Its high ceiling was blackened and its architectural ornaments lay in pieces on the floor. The cutting-edge cyberbodies that had been displayed along the walls and in the center of the hall gave no hint of their former shapes.

Two figures stood in the billowing clouds of black smoke.

"Freeze!"

At the sound of the explosion, eight armed guards came charging into the room.

One of them spotted the devastation outside the building's entrance. The four guards who had been watching the front doors lay dead on the ground. All of their heads had been ripped from their bodies, despite the fact that they were outfitted with peak-performance cyberbodies. Their guns were still holstered; it had happened before they'd even noticed the attacker.

The two figures were still.

They were carrying something on their backs, and they seemed to be wearing shoulder bags, too.

One of them let down his shoulder bag and reached into it.

"Shoot!" one of the guards commanded, and a volley of fire erupted from their handguns. They were trained to fire without hesitation if someone made a suspicious move.

The white smoke of the guns mixed with the black smoke from the explosion that filled the entrance foyer.

Then the armed guards stopped shooting.

Their handguns were loaded with 5.56 mm high-velocity armor-piercing bullets. Together, the eight men had fired a total of 136 shots at their target.

Normally, that would have done the trick.

But it hadn't.

Behind the curtain of smoke, the figure continued to move.

Calmly, it drew something out of the bag and connected it to some sort of belt attached to its back.

A heavy blast shook the entrance.

One of the armed guards was reduced to a piece of meat.

The weapon the figure was carrying was beyond the realm of the handgun.

A General Electric M-134.

Nicknamed "Old Painless," it was a mini-gun with rotating barrels.

Indeed, the guard who had just been pulverized had probably died before he had felt any pain.

The gun roared.

Its six barrels rotated, delivering more than one hundred 7.62 mm bullets per second.

The eight armed guards were blown to smithereens in less than a second.

A mountain of shell casings formed at the figure's feet as a belt fed the bullets stored in the knapsack to the M143.

As the gun smoke and the black cloud from the explosion began to clear, the figure's face became visible.

Tegan Yō, cyborg mercenary.

"This cyberbody is incredible. How did they cram this much power into an ordinary-sized body?" Yō marveled.

"It's made by Toyoda Chemical, the global leader. Toyoda really created exactly what I wanted."

"How romantic—using Toyoda-made cyberbodies to bring down the Toyoda empire."

"I suppose it is."

"Personally, I'm more than happy to get revenge on the company that used my body for its experiments to develop military cyberbodies with the SDF. Of course, the fact that I'm wearing one of their own loathsome creations to do it is almost a little bit too perfect."

The other man eyed the staircase. "Let's go. We don't want to keep them waiting."

Yō pointed at the elevator bank. "We're not taking the elevator?"

"With these cyberbodies? We'd fall through the floor."

"Good point."

Yō hung the minigun over his neck and shoulder with a sling, holstering the Vz83 submachine gun he had also drawn out of the bag.

"Come on," the man said.

Yō followed him towards the staircase.

"It's started," Batou mumbled bitterly.

The explosion had shaken Toyoda Chemical's entrance just as Section 9's Tiltorotor had landed on the building's roof.

"I'm glad we put that transmitter on Old Man Toyoda."

"Yes," she agreed.

"Tachikomas, are you ready?" Kusanagi called as she prepared for descent.

In the Tiltorotor's storage area, the Tachikomas raised their arms. <*Almost!*>

"Ishikawa! Remove the Tachikomas safety devices!"

"I'm on it!" Ishikawa detached the artillery covers of the Tachikomas grenade launchers.

<*Woo-hoo! It's been a while since we've been able to let these babies rip!*>

<Finally, we can exercise our true purpose as tanks!>

"This isn't a war. In five minutes, the prefectural police and Ground SDF will arrive to investigate the explosion. We need to secure the perps as well as Nakajima and Toyoda and make tracks before that happens. You have the position information for the inside of the building, right? Let's go!"

"Roger!"

Section 9's members and nine Tachikomas stormed the Toyoda Chemical building.

"Hello? Is there anybody there?"

At a terminal in the CEO's office, Nakajima was attempting to summon the guards.

There was no answer.

"Shit!"

Nakajima slammed the terminal down and began to collect his belongings.

Behind him, Toyoda spoke. "Where are you going?"

Nakajima looked at him.

"I'm getting out of here."

Just as his hand touched the door, it swung open from the other side.

Two men wearing helmets, goggles, and combat gear charged into the room, pointing their guns at Nakajima and Toyoda.

"Yikes!" Nakajima blurted, dropping his bag.

Toyoda raised his arms, exhibiting complete surrender.

One of the men lowered his gun and removed his goggles.

"It's you!" Toyoda exclaimed inadvertently.

"Please excuse me. My name is Togusa, of Public Safety Section 9. You're in danger here. Armed attackers are in the building."

Nakajima spoke. "Armed attackers!? Who are they?"

The other man removed his goggles. It was Paz. "There are two of them. They have military cyberbodies. You're their target."

"They're using our cyberbodies?!" Nakajima shrieked.

"Exactly. We have a Tiltorotor on the roof. We'll fly you out of here. Hurry!"

They had climbed sixty flights before coming to a door with a B mark on its door. "Wait," the man said, stopping suddenly

Up ahead, Yō stopped, too. "What is it?"

" . . . Somebody's here."

Yō peered into the hallway.

There was nobody there.

"I bet it's Public Safety Section 9," the man snarled.

"Section 9? So they were the ones from the run-in on the highway, too?"

"Yeah."

" . . . Got it. I'll go check it out. You're the boss, after all. You stay here."

Slowly, Yō began to make his way down the hallway.

He sensed a movement behind him.

Without turning, he unholstered his Vz83 with his left hand and squeezed the trigger.

The bullet ricocheted off of thin air.

"Huh?"

Yō turned to look.

Instantly, a barrage of grenade fire issued forth from behind him—but Yō's six-barrel mini-gun roared, detonating the grenade artillery before it reached him.

A curtain of fire swept through the corridor.

The flames shook the air, disrupting the effects of the thermoptic camouflage.

<I think he saw us!>

A Tachikoma was behind the grenade fire.

Its type 2909 thermoptic camouflage was rendered ineffectual by the heat of the grenade fire and the cloud of fine debris that filled the air.

The mini-gun unleashed another round.

<YIPES!>

The Tachikoma's round body dodged the bullets. But it knew that if the assault continued, it wouldn't be able to hold out for long.

<Oh, no you don't!>

Another Tachikoma behind Yō fired the machine gun installed in its manipulator.

The Tachikoma under the minigun's fire joined in with its machine gun, too.

It was a sublime exchange of fire—a battle of assured destruction.

"Tanks, huh? Hardly an even match," Yō muttered, turning down the passageway to the stairs.

The two Tachikomas raced after him.

<Wait up!>

When the Tachikomas turned the corner, they found themselves face to face with a second military cyborg, this one armed with a rocket cannon in his right hand.

<Anti-tank rockets!>

The military cyborg's right arm spewed fire. Then the sides of the arm split open to deliver a blast of gas.

At the same instant, a rocket warhead launched towards the Tachikomas, accelerating as it flew.

The Tachikomas fled in a panic.

The rocket hit a wall, blasting an enormous hole in the side of the building.

The man put away the rocket launcher in his right arm and urged Yō on.

"Let's go. Hurry."

That was when they heard the sound of an explosion overhead.

Just as the two men looked up, the stairway began to collapse, and a maelstrom of concrete and iron rubble rained down on them. They were enveloped in a dense cloud of dust.

Batou looked down at the mountain of debris.

He had blown away five flights of the staircase.

"Aw, did I overdo it again? That ought to hold 'em for a while."

As if in response, the debris began to shift.

"You've gotta be kidding!"

A barrage of mini-gun fire emanated from the pile of rubble and whizzed right by Batou's head.

A cloud of plaster showered down from the ceiling.

Then the mountain of debris exploded.

When the two men emerged from the flames, their skin was burnt to a crisp, but the wreckage around them had been blown away.

"What were you thinking, using rocket artillery at point-blank to clear the way?" Yō exclaimed.

The man brushed the dust from his cyberbody and looked up.

"We have to hurry or they'll get away."

The man leapt into the air, clung to the wall, and leapt again.

Rhythmically, he made his way up to the sixty-first, sixty-second, and sixty-third, and sixty-fourth floors.

With each jump, he gained nearly twenty meters in altitude.

When he reached the sixty-fifth floor, a powerful blast pelted the man from the hallway.

The shot knocked him back down to the rubble-strewn sixty-third floor, where Yō was.

"What happened?"

The man stood up in the wreckage. There was a huge hole in the middle of his torso. The man examined it dispassionately.

"Anti-material rifle. 12.7 mm. Huh. The chest armor on this thing is weaker than I thought."

The man faced Yō. "They're lying in wait for us on the sixty-fifth floor."

"That puts us at a disadvantage," Yō said, gazing upward.

On the sixty-fifth floor, Saito sat up after pulling the trigger of his anti-material rifle, which was bolted to the floor of the corridor.

"What's the deal? This thing can blast through tank armor!"

Batou was standing next to the demolished staircase. "They're freakishly tough. Major, lend us a Tachikoma, will you?" he cybercommed Kusanagi.

<Roger. Ishikawa and Borma are up to their necks. Togusa's group hasn't made it to the roof yet. Hold them off just a little longer.>

"Got it." Batou answered. He turned to Saito. "We'll just have to target their weaknesses."

"Weaknesses?"

"Can you blast off the plug covers on the back of their necks?"

"If they're facing away from us, I'd risk blowing out the whole plug. I could do it if they turn sideways."

"That's a pretty tall order. I'll see what I can do. Work your magic, sniper!"

"Be careful now, ranger!"

"Here he comes!"

They heard the sound of an impact against the wreckage.

Saito activated his type 2902 thermoptic camouflage.

Yō made his leap from the stairwell onto the sixty-fifth floor.

"What, no welcome party?"

Just as Yō aimed his mini-gun at the corridor where Saito was lying in wait, Batou deactivated his thermoptic camouflage and leapt in from Yō's right, kicking up the side of the mini-gun.

The mini-gun was thrust sideways, spraying holes in the wall and ceiling.

"That's a dangerous toy you've got there."

Batou pounced, using his brute force to yank off the mini-gun's belt.

"How do you like—"

But before he could say "them apples," he found himself looking down the barrel of a Vz83.

He turned his head, dodging the shot.

The bullet grazed the side of his face.

In the same motion, he spun his body and launched a forceful high-kick toward Yō's head.

Yō blocked it with his shoulder.

It was like kicking solid rock.

Yō swung his mini-gun down toward Batou's body.

Batou twisted his body to dodge the blow, stomping down on the minigun in Yō's right hand with his foot while using his right hand to hold down the Vz83 in Yō's left.

The full brunt of the military cyborg's strength raged against him. Then, for a brief moment, Yō was still.

"Saito!" Batou bellowed. "GO!!!"

The rifle fired. Its 12.7 mm bullet shot off the plug cover of Yō's cyberbody.

Batou had reached his limit.

With tremendous force, Yō flung Batou away.

Batou didn't resist. Instead, he used his feet to spring off of Yō's right arm and somersaulted in the air, crashing down onto Yō's head.

Yō's Vz83 began to move, but Batou was faster.

Withdrawing a cable from his hip, he stabbed it into the plug in the back of Yō's neck.

"Nighty-night."

Yō's eyes reflected Batou's triumphant smile.

For a brief moment, the mercenary's body stiffened, then crumpled to the floor with a thud.

Batou peered into Yō's face. "You were a pain in the ass, you know that? What's this 'Twins' business, anyway? Major, I've got his cyberbody code. I'm sending it to you—"

Just then, Yō's eyes rolled wildly in their sockets.

At an altitude of three hundred feet, the lounge commanded a panoramic view of the city lights.

Reinforced glass windows encircled the large, open floorplan, creating the illusion that the room was floating in the sky.

It was one of the more impressive features of Toyoda Chemical's headquarters.

Right now, however, the lounge's occupants were in no state to admire the view.

Not when life and death hung in the balance.

Only a flight of stairs stood between them and the roof.

Beyond those stairs, a Section 9 Tiltorotor awaited them.

Just a little bit further . . .

The stairway was visible next to the elevator in the center of the lounge.

Kusanagi was poised at the base of the stairs.

"This way!"

Togusa and Paz looked back down the stairway they had come up, brandishing their Sebros.

"Quick, go on ahead," Togusa told Toyoda and Nakajima. "We'll hold them off."

The staircase to the roof was less than twenty meters away.

Just then, the elevator began to move.

The light moved rapidly across the panel that indicated the elevator's floor.

The two men stopped in their tracks.

Kusanagi moved in front of the elevator, her Sebro 26A at the ready. "If you run, you'll make it. Go!" she shouted.

As if propelled by her voice, the two men took off running.

The elevator's floor indicator was just approaching the fortieth floor.

Suddenly, an explosion shook the other elevator, sending its doors flying. They made an ear-shattering noise as they skidded across the floor.

From the dark abyss of the elevator shaft, a figure emerged and blasted Kusanagi into space.

"—Uff!!"

She didn't even have time to parry.

Kusanagi's body soared through the air. She crashed through the lounge's glass wall, tumbling out into the sky.

"MAJOR!" Togusa shouted from the emergency staircase.

A stream of fire spurted toward Togusa from the elevator, and the ceiling over his head exploded.

Chunks of ceiling rained down, cutting Togusa and Paz off from the room.

It all took place in a split second.

What the . . . ?

Before they knew what was happening, Toyoda and Nakajima were laid out on the floor, unable to get up. More accurately, their legs gave out beneath them and they were too petrified to move.

"Finally, there's no one here to bother us."

The voice came from the elevator. They looked toward it.

The man was wearing a military cyberbody. His face was a standard, commercially available men's model.

Nakajima's voice quavered. "W-who are you?"

"Yōji Sakazaki. Also known as Yōji Tadayama."

"Tadayama . . . !" After his initial exclamation of surprise, Nakajima was rendered speechless.

"That's right. The son of the former Minister Tadayama, the man you framed and murdered!"

Sakazaki walked slowly toward the stunned Nakajima.

"So, Mr. Nakajima. You were on top of the world, weren't you? CEO of Toyoda Chemical, with a nice thick pipeline to your cronies in politics and finance. Did you think it was your own merits that brought you all that?"

Nakajima was as white as a sheet. He seemed unable to answer.

"Unfortunately, Mr. Nakajima, even coupled with your status as a founding member, your meager talents would have earned you a seat on the board of directors at the very most. But with me working for Kinoshita, you were raking it in, weren't you? You can thank me for your business tie-up with Narashino Technobody."

"T-that was Masumoto's . . . "

"Masumoto did whatever I told him. I suppose he believed

that a tie-up would lead to the development of better cybernetic technology. He believed that if the company changed, you could produce custom prosthetics that met the needs of the user, rather than manufacturing unit products that required the users to do the adapting. A truly noble man, that Masumoto. Not like you scumbags."

"What do you want from me, Sakazaki?"

Sakazaki laughed. "Revenge. I wanted to knock you down from your throne. I've worked towards this for fifteen long years!"

"Fifteen years—"

"I gave up everything. I invested all of my time. I went from cyberbody to cyberbody, changing identities—I was extremely thorough. I played so many roles, I didn't even have time to warm up the cold cyberbodies. Do you know how cold an unused cyberbody is? That coldness has frozen me to the very core."

Sakazaki crouched over Nakajima.

"My father was an admirable man. He had honor. He would never do anything underhanded. But you and Kinoshita scorned him and murdered him!"

He seized Nakajima by the collar and picked him up. Nakajima's feet dangled in the air.

"I can't . . . breathe . . . "

"How does it feel? I've suffered far worse, my entire life."

"P-please—"

"My father begged, too, didn't he? I know everything. I know you and Kinoshita called my father out to talk the night he died. The police didn't believe me—they thought my testimony was ridiculous. Only one detective listened to me. But you snuffed him out, didn't you?"

He flung Nakajima back down.

"Well, Nakajima? It's time for you to confess your sins."

Sakajima looked at Toyoda.

"You, too, Mr. Toyoda."

"Why me? I'm no longer employed here."

"You should have gone public with what you knew when you left the company. Instead, you ran away. That was the last straw. And that's not all! What about the recall order that Mr. Nakajima and Kinoshita squelched? I've seen hordes of people shed bitter tears over the defects in those cyberbodies. You have, too, haven't you, Mr. Toyoda? You witnessed their suffering firsthand in the Refugee Zone, didn't you?"

Toyoda was unable to respond.

"Time's up."

Sakazaki's right arm split open. He inserted a rocket shell in the arm and fired it toward the lounge's windows.

A streak of heat blazed over the two men's heads.

The immense pane of glass behind them exploded, splintering into a million shards.

The air in the lounge began to pour out into the void.

"I'd like to request that you apologize to the people of the world as you jump."

Nakajima and Toyoda gazed out into the sky.

The night air carried Sakajima's eerie voice.

"Right about now, the media probably gathered down below to investigate the explosions. They're being kind enough to broadcast our little event to the entire nation."

Through the broken window, they could see a helicopter hovering in the distance.

Nakajima spoke. "What about Kinoshita? Why should I be the one to die?"

"Kinoshita will witness your fate and rue his deeds as he waits in terror for his impending demise. Rest assured—I'll see to it that he pays his dues. You can leap to your death without worrying about that." Sakazaki smiled.

"All right . . . " Toyoda murmured.

He stood up. With the help of his crutches, he made his way toward the window.

"Wait!" Nakajima shouted.

Toyoda glanced back at him. "We were blind. I thought that if we could make a good product, we could bring people happiness. But that was just self-satisfaction. It's not about making a good product. It's about making a product that the customer needs. I didn't see that."

Nakajima let out a groan.

He stood up and began to walk.

The two men stood at the edge of the room.

The black sky stretched out beneath them.

One stood in fear, the other in regret.

The powerful wind whipped past them.

The two men shut their eyes tightly and leaped out into space.

An indescribable smile stretched across Sakazaki's face.

A cybercomm flashed in.

<*Yō speaking.*> Yō's voice resonated in Sakazaki's cyberbrain.

"—Did you wrap things up?"

<Yeah. Did you?>

"Mission accomplished. Now we just have to make our escape."

<Right . . . >

"The signal's awfully weak . . . I'm getting some static, too."

<Yeah. I'm transmitting from my second brain. They stuck a cyberbrain lock on the first one.>

"I see."

<I have one request. I want to see Nakajima and Toyoda's bodies for myself.>

"Fair enough. You're entitled to that. You can use my eyes."

Sakazaki walked to the edge of the room.

He looked down.

Far, far below, he could see two tiny blotches, like two black flowers blooming on the concrete.

Sakazaki smiled.

"Like death flowers for Kinoshita."

<Really! Is that what you see, asshole?>

"What!"

As the exclamation left his lips, Sakazaki's body doubled over as if struck by an electric shock. He fell to the floor.

Static entered his vision as his visual field was overwritten.

Now he saw a Tachikoma perched on the side of the building, cradling Nakajima and Toyoda.

"ARRGGHHH!" Sakazaki roared. But his cyberbody refused to respond.

He felt something hard stab him in the back of the head.

A voice spoke to him from above.

"Don't bother. I've fried all of the links to your motor nerves. Too bad your fancy military cyberbody doesn't make your cyberbrain invulnerable."

It was Kusanagi.

She dangled by a wire from another Tachikoma perched on the side of the building, holding an anti-material rifle.

"Our brains! How did you . . . " Sakazaki asked.

<*We used cybercomms to wash a control virus into your cyberbodies,*> Batou's voice said.

On the sixty-fifth floor, Batou was transmitting through a cable connected to the second brain he had plucked out of Yō's body.

<*I never figured that Yō had two brains shells. So that's why they called him 'Twins.' I pulled the brain shell out of his stomach and used it to chat with you suckers. A convincing performance, don't you think?*>

"My p-plans . . . you've ruined everything . . . "

"I have a lot of questions for your brain shells, you two," Kusanagi said icily. "I want to hear the full story of the collusion between Kinoshita and Toyoda Chemical."

Sakazaki screamed soundlessly. His voice reverberated only in his own mind, never shaking the vocal cords of his cyberbody.

A cry of something between lament and rage.

Chapter 10

The day after the incident at Toyoda Chemical, Nana Kirishima stood in front of a gravestone in a cemetery flooded with the orange light of the setting sun.

Detective Kirishima's name was inscribed on the stone.

She hung her head as she lingered, wordlessly.

"I figured you would be here, on the anniversary of Detective Kirishima's death," a voice said suddenly.

She looked up.

Standing on the thin path between the lines of gravestones was the woman called Kusanagi she had met at the police station. Behind her was the robot Kirishima had come to be fond of, though it was painted a different color now.

<*Long time no see!*>

"Tachikoma-chan!"

"There's just one thing I want to ask you before I leave you to your tearful reunion . . . " Kusanagi's steely voice interrupted the emotional moment. She held up a notebook for Kirishima to see.

"Thanks to Detective Kirishima's journal, it looks like we're going to be able to uncover the ties between Kinoshita and Nakajima of Toyoda Chemical. You have our gratitude."

Kirishima shook her head. "There's no need to thank me. I'm the one who's grateful to you."

"Actually, we'd like to present you with a certificate of appreciation. But that's not why I'm here today."

"I'm ready. That's why I came here today . . . to tell my father."

"I see. In that case—" Kusanagi's expression turned severe. "Nana Kirishima. I'd like to ask you to come in for voluntary questioning on suspicion of aiding and abetting the abduction of Kin'ichi Masumoto, executive director of Toyoda Chemical."

Kirishima gave a small nod of assent and moved away from Detective Kirishima's grave.

"Tachikoma, supervise Nana Kirishima."

<Roger!>

The Tachikoma moved behind Kirishima and began to walk.

Still facing forward, Kirishima began to talk, almost as if to herself.

"Back when I first went cybernetic, I resented this cold body of mine. But now I finally understand. It wasn't my body that was cold—it was my heart. You were the one who helped me to realize, Tachikoma-chan: even a machine can be warm."

Both the Tachikoma and Kusanagi listened silently to Kirishima's words.

Kirishima wasn't seeking a response to what she was saying. Right now, she just wanted to express exactly how she was feeling.

In the empty graveyard, the tombstone faded from orange to the color of dusk.

Chapter 11

When word got out that Toyoda Chemical's license to produce military cyberbodies was linked to hefty political contributions exchanged by CEO Nakajima and Representative Kinoshita—leader of the faction known as the second power of the ruling party—the news sent shockwaves through political and industry circles.

Further intrigue rocked society when the same parties were arrested in connection to the mysterious death of Health, Labor, and Welfare Minister Tadayama fifteen years ago. The fact that the two suspects were apprehended just as the statute of limitations was about to expire unleashed a rash of speculative rumors.

Back at Section 9 headquarters, Kusanagi sat on the sofa in front of Aramaki's desk.

"It was really Sakazaki's testimony and the accounts in Detective Kirishima's journal of being shunted from one prefectural police force to the next before he was killed that enabled us to arrest those two," Kusanagi remarked.

"True. It was the persistence of one man bent on vengeance, and another man determined to pursue the truth to his death."

"But the real catalyst was Sakazaki's preemptive strike against Section 9 when he hired that sniper to try to make sure we wouldn't get in his way," she pointed out.

"If you look at it that way, throughout these incidents Sakazaki played us like puppets, to enact his own revenge," Aramaki mused.

"When Kirishima became acquainted with Sakazaki through the Toyoda Chemical Cybernetics Victims Group, she agreed to participate in Masumoto's abduction not for vengeance, but out of the desire to learn the truth. And when Masumoto was abducted, I'm sure he was confused, but he let Sakazaki strong-arm him into doing a brain-shell swap. Sakazaki was under orders from Kinoshita when he plotted the chief's assassination, but in fact he was motivated by his own agenda: preventing us from foiling his revenge. It was the subtle links between each party's motives that set the entire string of events in motion," Kusanagi concluded.

"I suppose that those subtle forces are still smoldering in the bowels of this city," Aramaki said ominously.

"Probably," Kusanagi agreed, gazing out at the city of Niihama through the window.

The world was flooded with darkness.

Perhaps that darkness harbored untold malice.

Perhaps that malice would again spawn actors like Sakazaki.

They had to cast light into the obscurity, identify the seeds of iniquity, and stamp them out.

If they could prevent even some of those evils from taking root, they might be able to prevent people like Kirishima and Sakazaki from being victimized in the future.

"We'll just have to continue our work until the day we're no longer needed." Kusanagi smiled at Aramaki.

Afterword

I hope you enjoyed *Revenge of the Cold Machines,* the second installment of the Stand Alone Complex novels series. After the publication of *The Last Memory,* many readers expressed the desire for more Tachikoma involvement, even reproaching me for not including them more. It was clear that the fans wanted to hear more about the Tachikomas, so I have devoted more than a quarter of the new book to the Tachikomas' escapades.

The story for the second book also comes from a slant on the refugee issue that is one of the themes of the TV anime *Stand Alone Complex: 2nd Gig.* I aspired to create a sense of the refugees' circumstances by creating continuities with the script I wrote for the *2nd Gig* "Excavation" episode.

The television broadcasts of the *2nd Gig* have passed the halfway mark and the story is building toward its climax. After I tossed them my finished script, shouting, "Do your stuff, Director Kamiyama!" I sat back to enjoy the rest of the season as a member of the viewing audience. The unfortunate part is that I know how the story will develop, so unless Director Kanji Kamiyama pulls a fast one on the scriptwriting team and completely rewrites the story, I know what to expect. I'm deprived of that aspect of the show, but I do get to enjoy seeing how the episodes have been animated. This is a special pleasure only afforded to people involved with the creation process.

Of course, the scripts are written with the animation in mind, so we can't write about things that can't be drawn. For example, it's easy to write the words "Ten thousand military cyborgs attack Kusanagi," but if we give that to an artist to illustrate, they'll probably refuse to ever work with us again.

That's precisely why novels can be compelling in ways that visual imagery cannot. For that reason, I tried to write each scene in such a way that the readers would be able to picture what was happening, but I think there are also aspects I incorporated *because* of the fact that they weren't illustratable. I hope you enjoyed Stand Alone Complex in this text format.

Right now, my Stand Alone Complex work has quieted down a bit and I'm taking part in the scriptwriting of Production I.G's next project, a television animated series called *Otogizoushi*. The first episode will be aired around the time this novel lands in bookstores. I intended to write three scripts and be done with it, just to tide myself over until my next project, but the series producer Yoshiki Sakurai managed to trick me into allowing it to become my main focus. President Mitsuhisa Ishikawa and Mr. Mamoru Oshii roped me in when I first started working on Stand Alone Complex, and now I'm even being roped in by my underlings! Up until now I've allowed myself to be blown this way and that, but I'm beginning to think that it might be time for me to take more of a proactive stance in deciding what direction to take with my work.

For that reason, I plan to begin devising the plot for my third Ghost in the Shell book very soon.

Junichi Fujisaku
Production I.G Studio
June 2004

About the author

Born on August 6, 1967, JUNICHI FUJISAKU was one of the first graduates of the Oshii Academy, an in-studio think-tank created by acclaimed director Mamoru Oshii at the animation house Production I.G to train the next generation of writers, directors, and animators. Currently the Chief Director and scriptwriter for the Game Production Department of Production I.G Fujisaku has also written almost a dozen episodes of the *Ghost in the Shell: Stand Alone Complex* television series, as well as co-developing Blood the Last Vampire, for which he was the director of the videogame version as well as writing one of the Blood novels and directing *Blood+*, the new television series, and the series *Yarudora*.

About the cover artists

Born March 4, 1968 in the Niigata Prefecture, KAZUTO NAKAZAWA (front cover artist) is an animator and illustrator. His major works include character design on *El Hazard: The Magnificent World; Legend of Black Heaven; Ashita no Nadja;* and *Samurai Champloo*. He also directed the anime portion of *Kill Bill Volume 1*, and was the key animator of "A Detective Story," a short film in *The Animatrix*.

Ryouta Niino (*Back cover*)
Born January 13, 1973. Animator. Art director for *Ghost in the Shell: Stand Alone Complex* and *Ghost in the Shell: S.A.C 2nd Gig*.